Best Easy Day Hikes
Rocky Mountain National Park

Help Us Keep This Guide Up to Date

The authors and editors have made every effort to make this guide as accurate and useful as possible; however, many things can change after a guide is published—regulations change, facilities come under new management, and so forth.

We would love to hear from you concerning your experiences with this guide and how you feel it could be improved and kept up to date. While we may not be able to respond to all comments and suggestions, we'll take them to heart, and we'll also make certain to share them with the author. Please send your comments and suggestions to 64 South Main Street, Essex, Connecticut 06426.

Thanks for your input!

Best Easy Day Hikes Series

Best Easy Day Hikes Rocky Mountain National Park

Fourth Edition

Kent Dannen and Susan Joy Paul

ESSEX, CONNECTICUT

FALCONGUIDES®

An imprint of The Globe Pequot Publishing Group, Inc.
64 South Main Street
Essex, CT 06426
www.globepequot.com

Falcon and FalconGuides are registered trademarks and Make Adventure Your Story is a trademark of The Globe Pequot Publishing Group, Inc.

Copyright © 2026 by The Globe Pequot Publishing Group, Inc.

Maps by The Globe Pequot Publishing Group, Inc.

All rights reserved. No part of this book may be reproduced in any form or by any electronic or mechanical means, including information storage and retrieval systems, without written permission from the publisher, except by a reviewer who may quote passages in a review.

British Library Cataloguing in Publication Information available

Library of Congress Cataloging-in-Publication Data Available

ISBN 978-1-4930-8780-8 (paperback)
ISBN 978-1-4930-8781-5 (ebook)

> The authors and The Globe Pequot Publishing Group, Inc., assume no liability for accidents happening to, or injuries sustained by, readers who engage in the activities described in this book.

Contents

Introduction 1
Trail Finder 13
Map Legend 16

Beaver Meadows Entrance and Bear Lake Corridor (Estes Park)

1 Bear Lake 18
2 Nymph Lake, Dream Lake, and Emerald Lake 21
3 Lake Haiyaha 25
4 Flattop Mountain 29
5 Alberta Falls 33
6 The Loch 36
7 Mills Lake 39
8 Bierstadt Lake 42
9 Sprague Lake 45
10 Cub Lake 49
11 Fern Lake 52
12 Spruce Lake 56

Fall River Entrance and East Side of Trail Ridge Road (Estes Park)

13 Chipmunk Lake and Ypsilon Lake 60
14 Horseshoe Falls 63
15 Chasm Falls 66
16 Roger Toll Memorial 69
17 Deer Mountain 73

Kawuneeche Entrance and West Side of Trail Ridge Road (Grand Lake)

18 Big Meadows and Granite Falls 77
19 Coyote Valley 80
20 Lulu City Site 83
21 Mount Ida 87

Wild Basin Entrance (Allenspark)

22 Sandbeach Lake 91
23 Ouzel Falls.. 94
24 Bluebird Lake 98

Other Entrances and Trailheads

25 West Creek Falls 103
26 Bridal Veil Falls 106
27 Gem Lake.. 110
28 MacGregor Falls 113
29 Lily Lake... 116
30 Peacock Pool and Columbine Falls............................... 119
31 Cascade Falls and North Inlet Falls 122
32 Adams Falls... 126
33 Lone Pine Lake and Lake Verna 129

About the Authors 133

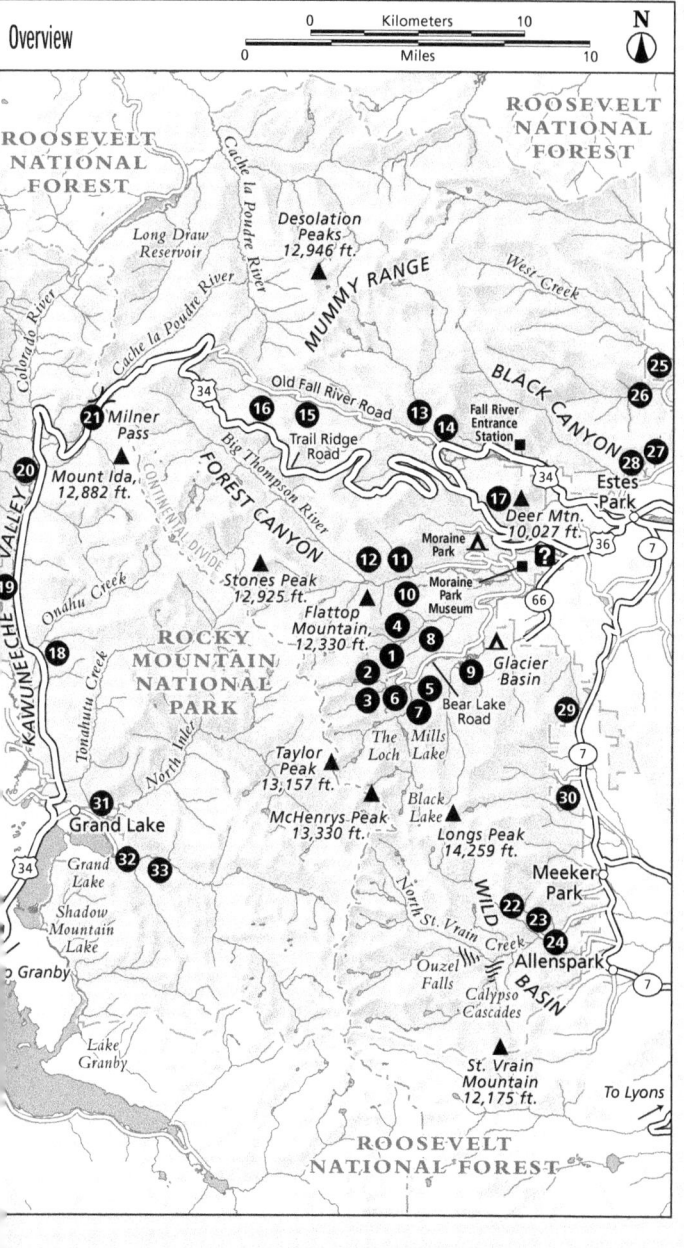

Introduction

Rocky Mountain National Park lies just sixty-five miles northwest of Denver, yet worlds apart from the hustle and bustle of Colorado's state capital. Home to dozens of lakes, waterfalls, and mountains, including the iconic Longs Peak, the 415-square-mile national park boasts over 300 miles of hiking trails, allowing intrepid visitors access to a plethora of natural wonders.

Park Entrances, Passes, and Seasonal Timed Entry

Visitors to the main park area are invited to enter from four locations: at the eastern edge, from Beaver Meadows and Fall River Entrance Stations, situated west of Estes Park; at the southeast end, from Wild Basin Entrance Station, located north of Allenspark; and from the southwest side at Kawuneeche Entrance Station, north of Grand Lake.

At the entrance station, you must show an ID and a park pass. Purchase a one-day or seven-day individual, motorcycle, or vehicle pass, or an annual pass online at www.recreation.gov/sitepass/74291 or use your credit or debit card to buy one at the entrance station. Note that cash and checks are not accepted. You can also access the park with an America the Beautiful Pass. Some, but not all, other Interagency passes are also accepted.

A park pass does not guarantee admission. In addition, you may also need a reservation. From mid-October to mid-May, reservations are not required. From mid-May to mid-October, access to Rocky Mountain National Park is by a timed-entry reservation system. Due to the popularity of the Bear Lake area, timed-entry reservations are available with and without access to Bear Lake Road. If you've already visited that lake and the surrounding hiking trails, including Moraine Park, Sprague Lake, and the Glacier Gorge Trailhead, and revisiting them is not a top priority, consider excluding access, and you may find more times available.

Since timed-entry times, dates, and rules may change from year to year, you are strongly advised to visit the timed-entry permit system website for the most up-to-date information. Plan ahead and avoid being turned away at the entrance gate. Call 877-444-6777 or check the park's timed entry site at www.nps.gov/romo/planyourvisit/timed-entry-permit-system.htm and reserve your time slot at www.recreation.gov/timed-entry/10086910.

Trail Ridge Road and Old Fall River Road are closed to through traffic seasonally, depending on snow conditions. If you plan to enter the park from the Kawuneeche Entrance Station, near Grand Lake, or plan to recreate on trails from Trail Ridge Road during the seasonal closure, call the Trail Ridge Road recorded phone line at 970-586-1222 for status updates.

Rocky Mountain National Park areas beyond the main park are accessed via several trailheads not accessible through the main entrance gates, and entry requirements vary. These include the East Longs Peak Trailhead, Lumpy Ridge Trailhead, Cow Creek Trailhead, and Lily Lake Trailhead, among others. These trailheads do not provide access to the main park by hiking trails.

On-Site Resources and Restrictions

There are no restaurants, grocery stores, or food vendors in the park. Bring your own food, consume it in your vehicle or in designated picnic areas, and pack out everything or dispose of it in a trash receptacle. If you leave food or coolers in your vehicle while you hike, cover them so as not to attract wildlife.

There are no gas stations in Rocky Mountain National Park. Fill your tank in nearby Estes Park, Grand Lake, or Allenspark. You may be driving a lot within the park, so don't enter Rocky Mountain National Park without adequate fuel.

Pets are not allowed on any trails, meadows, or tundra. They are not allowed in the visitor centers. They are allowed on established roads and in some camping, parking, and picnic areas. You may not leave your pet tied up outside while you hike, so if you want to enjoy the trails and you have a pet, consider boarding them in a nearby facility before entering the park.

Rocky Mountain National Park is a special place. The general rule is to leave the place the way you found it or better by sticking to designated trails, packing out trash, and respecting other visitors' experiences.

Follow the seven Leave No Trace principles per lnt.org.

A complete list of rules and regulations may be found at: www.nps.gov/romo/planyourvisit/rules_regulations.htm

Wildlife

Ninety-four percent of the park is a designated wilderness area, protected from development and providing a magical habitat for more than 60 species of mammals and nearly 300 species of birds. In addition, many reptiles, amphibians, insects, and plants, including almost a thousand species of wildflowers, thrive within the boundaries of Rocky Mountain National Park.

Depending on the location and time of year, you may spot moose, elk, mule deer, coyotes, foxes, snowshoe hares, yellow-bellied marmots, pikas, chipmunks, red squirrels, golden-mantled ground squirrels, Richardson's ground squirrels, Merriam's turkeys, mallard ducks, ptarmigans, gray jays, ravens, Steller's jays, Clark's nutcrackers, water ouzels (also known as American dippers), water pipits, white-throated swifts, white-crowned sparrows, black-billed magpies, horned larks, mountain chickadees, butterflies, and much more wildlife along the roadways and on the trails. Though black bears inhabit the park, they are not common and are seldom spotted.

However, other large animals are common. Deer, especially, can be curious, and moose can be dangerous. Even small animals can carry diseases. Keep a safe distance, do not approach the wildlife, and never attempt to pet or feed animals in the park. Admire them from afar. Take pictures, but leave the wildlife alone.

Camping

Camping is available seasonally in Moraine Park Campground, Glacier Basin Campground, Timber Creek Campground, and Longs Peak Campground, and year-round in Aspenglen Campground. Seasonally, Moraine Park, Glacier Basin, Timber Creek, and Aspenglen campsites are by reservation only, and Longs Peak campsites are first-come, first-served. During the offseason, campsites in Aspenglen Campground are also first-come, first-served. Check the park's website at www.nps.gov/romo/planyourvisit

/camping.htm for rules, hours, fees, and resources, and reserve your campsite at www.recreation.gov.

If you have a reserved campsite in the Aspenglen, Moraine Park, Glacier Basin, or Timber Creek Campgrounds during a timed-entry period, you do not require a timed-entry permit and will be admitted into the park at the time of your campsite availability, 1 o'clock, on the first day of your reservation.

For backcountry camping, wilderness sites are available by permit. Check the website for details at www.nps.gov/romo/planyourvisit/wilderness-overnight-backpacking.htm.

Maps

Each hike in this book includes a map. For maps that cover larger areas, turn to the National Geographic Trails Illustrated Topographic Maps #200: Rocky Mountain National Park, #1701: Rocky Mountain National Park Day Hikes, and #301: Longs Peak: Rocky Mountain National Park [Bear Lake, Wild Basin]. These maps are available at outdoor retailers, park visitor centers, and online at www.natgeomaps.com/trail-maps/trails-illustrated-maps/colorado.

For maps covering smaller areas of the park in greater detail, US Geological Survey quadrangle maps are available at https://store.usgs.gov.

Though the hikes in this book are listed by region and the trails in Rocky Mountain National Park are often well signed, a larger, more comprehensive map will help you understand the overall layout of the park for a more efficient hiking plan.

Getting Around the Park

Trailheads and campgrounds in Rocky Mountain National Park are accessible by car. However, some tent sites, designated as walk-in sites, require a short walk from parking area to campsite.

Parking areas fill up quickly, especially during the peak summer season. Consider parking in Rocky Mountain National Park's Park and Ride lot and taking the free In-Park Shuttle, a fleet of buses that travels the Bear Lake Road Corridor with stops at popular trailheads including Bear Lake, Glacier Gorge, and Sprague Lake. Check the park website for a route map and days of service at www.nps.gov/romo/planyourvisit/shuttle-buses-and-public-transit.htm.

Trail Ridge Road, a high paved road that connects the west side of the park near Grand Lake to the east side near Estes Park, is closed seasonally. Old Fall River Road, a one-way gravel road that begins in Horseshoe Park near the Fall River entrance on the east side of the park and ends at Trail Ridge Road, is also closed to traffic seasonally. Bear this in mind when you plan your hikes. For example, if you enter the park at the Kawuneeche Entrance Station when Trail Ridge Road is closed, you will not have access to trails on the east side of the park. Depending on weather and snowfall, other roads in the park may be closed temporarily.

What's New in This Edition

This book has been revised since the third edition, written by Kent Dannen, was published in 2020. If you are familiar with that edition, you'll see the following changes in this one. You'll also see information that was simply verified and left intact:

- **The hikes are arranged by entrance station**: Beaver Meadows, Fall River, Kawuneeche, and Wild Basin, with a final section for trailheads outside these main entrance stations
- **Hike number, name, and short description**: Verified and updated as needed in each chapter
- **Distance**: Verified and updated as needed in each chapter
- **Hiking time**: Verified and updated as needed in each chapter. The times suggested are average times based on the distance, elevation gain, and difficulty of each hike. They do not reflect the hiking times of the authors. They also do not account for breaks to snack, snap photos, and take in the glory that is Rocky Mountain National Park. Your hiking times may be much shorter or longer.
- **Difficulty**: Verified and updated with regard to distance, elevation gain, and terrain. For the very fit hiker, every hike may be designated as "easy." However, since the park attracts people new to hiking, including visitors from lower elevations, the designations in each chapter have been updated to include degrees of "easiness," from "Very Easy" to "Easy," "Easy to Moderate," and "Easy to Strenuous." So a hike that's easy for one hiker may be strenuous for another hiker. If at any time a hike becomes too difficult, simply turn around and return to the trailhead.
- **Trail surface**: This information has been removed from each chapter, as nearly every hike is on dirt and some include occasional rocky sections, though none

are technical, and they do not require special gear to navigate. However, if you are visiting the park during the spring, winter, or fall, expect snow on the trails, especially at higher elevations. For this reason, trekking poles and boot traction such as MICROspikes are highly recommended from fall through spring, and even in the summer for higher elevation hikes such as Flattop Mountain.

- **Best season**: This information has also been removed, as the best season depends on the temperature, precipitation, humidity, snowfall, and your personal preferences. You'll find drier trails in the summer, but they'll be crowded. You'll find snow in the winter, but can enjoy the solitude. Many people enjoy the park in the spring and fall. The key to making every hike enjoyable is to set realistic expectations and prepare with proper clothing and gear for the season. For example, if there is snow on the trail, you may need boot traction, or even snowshoes.
- **Other trail users**: Verified and updated as needed in each chapter
- **Canine compatibility**: This information has been removed from each chapter. Dogs are not allowed on trails in Rocky Mountain National Park. You cannot leave them tied up outside while you hike, so if you plan to hike in the park, leave the pup at home.
- **Fees and permits**: This information has been removed from individual hikes. No matter where you enter, you must pay a park entrance fee. During timed-entry season, you must also have a timed-entry reservation. If you are entering the park from a trailhead outside the main park area, such as Lumpy Ridge, East Inlet Trail, North Inlet Trail, and other trailheads outside the main area, print out your reservation and display it on your

dashboard. Note that you can visit all areas of the park *except for the Bear Lake Corridor* without a timed-entry reservation year-round if you arrive before 9 a.m. or after 2 p.m., and you can visit the entire park *including the Bear Lake Corridor* if you arrive before 5 a.m. or after 6 p.m., Mountain Time.

- **Wildlife**: This has been removed from each chapter, as the wildlife travels throughout the park. Generally speaking, you are more likely to see wildlife in the more remote and less popular areas of the park, such as hikes on the west side of the park and those at higher elevations, and hikes near water. However, it is not uncommon for deer, elk, and even moose to enter popular, crowded areas, including campgrounds.
- **Trail contact**: This has been removed. The trail contact is the same for every hike: Rocky Mountain National Park Backcountry Office, 1000 US Hwy 36, Estes Park; (970) 586-1242; www.nps.gov/romo
- **Maps, Highlights, Trailhead and destination elevations, Finding the trailhead, The Hike, and Miles and Directions**: Verified and updated as needed in each chapter. Note that summit elevations for Flattop Mountain, Deer Mountain, and Mount Ida have been updated to reflect LiDAR technology elevations and may differ slightly from elevations displayed on USGS maps.
- **Several hikes have been removed, and new ones have been added.**

In addition, each **map**, the **Trail Finder**, and the **Map Legend** have been verified and updated, including the addition of "Best Hikes for Lakes" and "Best Hikes for Wheelchairs and Strollers" entries in the Trail Finder.

How to Use This Guide

This book includes thirty-three hikes to lakes, waterfalls, mountains, and other scenic destinations. The hikes are arranged by entrance station. No matter where you enter the park or which campground you choose to pitch your tent, you'll find hikes nearby.

You can select your hikes first and then pick the entrance station or wait until you've reserved a time slot or campsite and then take a look at the hikes nearby. The time slot matters, because if you are not able to reserve a permit that includes Bear Lake Road, all hikes in the Bear Lake Corridor will be off-limits. The campsite is less important, but choosing hikes close to your campground will save you driving-around time to trailheads.

Except for the Wild Basin entrance and entry points beyond the main park area, no matter where you enter, you can get just about anywhere in the park, barring roads such as Trail Ridge Road and Old Fall River Road closing for the season. For example, if you enter the park at the Beaver Meadows Entrance Station, you can still get to the trailheads in the Fall River Entrance section of the book. You'll just have a slightly longer drive.

The Trail Finder that follows this section recommends hikes by destination, such as lake, peak, or waterfall; by experience, such as best views; and by hiking participants, such as best hikes with children.

Each hike includes a description, start, distance, difficulty, trailhead and destination elevations, and other pertinent data to help you choose hikes that best suit your interests and ability. Trail surfaces, which are mostly dirt, vary from well-maintained and accessible by wheelchair to rocky, rugged, and exposed. Miles and directions are also included for easier route finding and to track your progress. Finally, a map is included for each hike, giving you a birds-eye view of the area.

Before You Go

- Check www.nps.gov/romo/ for alerts and road closures.
- Check www.nps.gov/romo/planyourvisit/trail_conditions.htm for trail conditions.
- Bring the right gear and clothing for the weather and trail conditions.
- If you are visiting during a timed-entry period, print out your reservation (for all entrances) or take a photo of the entire document with your phone so you can show it at the entrance gate (for main entrances only).
- If you are visiting Rocky Mountain National Park from a lower elevation, be prepared for symptoms of altitude sickness such as lightheadedness, nausea, and headache. Be sure to stay hydrated by drinking water regularly. Treat your symptoms with over-the-counter medications, and if they persist, stick to lower-elevation trails in the park.
- Fill your gas tank.
- Make sure you have enough food, water, and other beverages for your visit.
- If you're camping, ensure you have everything you need for an overnight stay, so you don't have to drive into town in the middle of the night.
- Be patient. Rocky Mountain National Park is a popular place and during the peak season, the staff is incredibly busy managing the influx of visitors seeking their own wilderness experience. Be kind to the rangers and other staff and to people at camp and on the trail.

- More questions? Call a Rocky Mountain National Park office:
  - Visitor Centers: (970) 586-1206
  - Wilderness Office: (970) 586-1242
  - Trail Ridge Road recorded information: (970) 586-1222

Trail Finder

Best Hikes for Great Views
  1 Bear Lake
  2 Nymph Lake, Dream Lake, and Emerald Lake
  4 Flattop Mountain
  6 The Loch
  9 Sprague Lake
 16 Roger Toll Memorial
 17 Deer Mountain
 21 Mount Ida
 24 Bluebird Lake
 30 Peacock Pool and Columbine Falls

Best Hikes for Lakes
  1 Bear Lake
  2 Nymph Lake, Dream Lake, and Emerald Lake
  3 Lake Haiyaha
  6 The Loch
  7 Mills Lake
  8 Bierstadt Lake
  9 Sprague Lake
 10 Cub Lake
 11 Fern Lake
 12 Spruce Lake
 13 Chipmunk Lake and Ypsilon Lake
 22 Sandbeach Lake
 24 Bluebird Lake
 27 Gem Lake
 29 Lily Lake
 30 Peacock Pool and Columbine Falls
 33 Lone Pine Lake and Lake Verna

Best Hikes for Waterfalls
  5 Alberta Falls

- 14 Horseshoe Falls
- 15 Chasm Falls
- 18 Big Meadows and Granite Falls
- 23 Ouzel Falls
- 25 West Creek Falls
- 26 Bridal Veil Falls
- 30 Peacock Pool and Columbine Falls
- 31 Cascade Falls and North Inlet Falls
- 32 Adams Falls

Best Hikes with Children
- 1 Bear Lake
- 5 Alberta Falls
- 9 Sprague Lake
- 14 Horseshoe Falls
- 16 Roger Toll Memorial
- 27 Gem Lake
- 29 Lily Lake
- 32 Adams Falls

Best Hikes for Wildlife
- 10 Cub Lake
- 18 Big Meadows and Granite Falls
- 21 Mount Ida
- 24 Bluebird Lake
- 26 Bridal Veil Falls

Best Hikes for Photographers
- 2 Nymph Lake, Dream Lake, and Emerald Lake
- 6 The Loch
- 7 Mills Lake
- 9 Sprague Lake
- 22 Sandbeach Lake
- 23 Ouzel Falls
- 24 Bluebird Lake

27 Gem Lake
30 Peacock Pool and Columbine Falls

Best Summit Hikes
 4 Flattop Mountain
17 Deer Mountain
21 Mount Ida

Best Hikes for Solitude
10 Cub Lake
13 Chipmunk Lake and Ypsilon Lake
18 Big Meadows and Granite Falls
24 Bluebird Lake
25 West Creek Falls
26 Bridal Veil Falls
31 Cascade Falls and North Inlet Falls
33 Lone Pine Lake and Lake Verna

Best Hikes for Wheelchairs and Strollers
 1 Bear Lake
 9 Sprague Lake
14 Horseshoe Falls
16 Roger Toll Memorial
19 Coyote Valley
29 Lily Lake

Map Legend

══⟨34⟩══	US Highway
══⟨278⟩══	State Highway
─────	Local Road
── ── ──	Unimproved Road
▬▬▬▬▬	Featured Trail
─ ─ ─ ─	Trail
── · ── · ──	Continental Divide
── · · ── · · ──	National Forest/Park Boundary
~~	River/Creek
⬭	Body of Water
⛺	Campground
⌶	Gate
▲	Mountain/Peak
🌲	Park
🅿	Parking
⌣	Pass
⊞	Picnic Area
■	Point of Interest/Structure
🏛	Ranger Station
🚻	Restrooms
❶	Trailhead
○	Town/City
👁	Viewpoint/Overlook
❓	Visitor/Information Center
≳	Waterfall

Beaver Meadows Entrance and Bear Lake Corridor (Estes Park)

1 Bear Lake

A mostly level path circles the park's most popular lake and provides a scenic backdrop for photos, with Hallett Peak rising above the lake and reflected in the water below.

Start: Bear Lake Trailhead
Hiking time: 30 minutes to 1 hour
Distance: 0.7-mile lollipop loop
Difficulty: Very easy
Other trail users: Wheelchairs, strollers
Maps: Trails Illustrated #200: Rocky Mountain National Park; USGS McHenrys Peak
Highlights: Views of Hallett Peak and Longs Peak, natural history points of interest
Elevations trailhead to Bear Lake: 9,457 feet to 9,475 feet (+18 feet)

Finding the trailhead: From the Beaver Meadows Entrance Station in Estes Park, drive 0.2 mile and turn left on Bear Lake Road. Continue 9.4 miles to the parking lot and trailhead at the road's end (GPS: 40 18.7177, -105 38.7584).

The Hike

The mostly level trail around Bear Lake is very popular. Nonetheless, it offers many opportunities for unspoiled views as well as photographs of the landscape, close-ups of patterns on tree trunks and boulders, wildlife portraits, and dramatic settings for people pictures.

Thirty-two numbered posts around the lake indicate points of interest, with short but informative descriptions in a booklet available from a dispenser at the east end of the lake. This reference is handy for anyone walking around Bear Lake. The more you know about what you see, the more likely you are to enjoy it and to notice things you otherwise might have overlooked.

Early morning is the best time to view the east end of the lake, where most people congregate. Arriving early will help you avoid crowds and also enable you to view shadowed trees and boulders in the foreground as interesting silhouettes framing rugged cliffs above.

Heading counterclockwise around the lake will give you the most opportunities for interesting views of Hallett Peak. Fences protect some areas from trampling feet; walkers should stay on the trail. Also along the east side of the lake, look for interesting grain patterns in weathered limber pines. Be sure to notice the patterns of gneiss, a type of rock pointed out at stop ten.

Around stop twelve are magnificent views across the lake to Longs Peak and the other high mountains surrounding Glacier Gorge. This perspective of Longs is best enjoyed in late afternoon. Any time of day, however, is a wonderful time to enjoy the beauty the Bear Lake area has to offer.

Miles and Directions

0.0 Start at the Bear Lake trailhead by the ranger station at the west side of the parking lot. Cross a bridge and bear right. At about 150 feet, reach a trail junction and the start of the loop hike. Go right on the trail. (Alternatively, go left to do the loop clockwise.)
0.1 Enjoy views of Hallett Peak above the lake.
0.4 Reach the lake's northwest corner and bend left on the trail along the lake's west shoreline. Stop for views south to Longs Peak. Continue around the lake to the junction and turn right to return to the trailhead.
0.7 Arrive back at the trailhead.

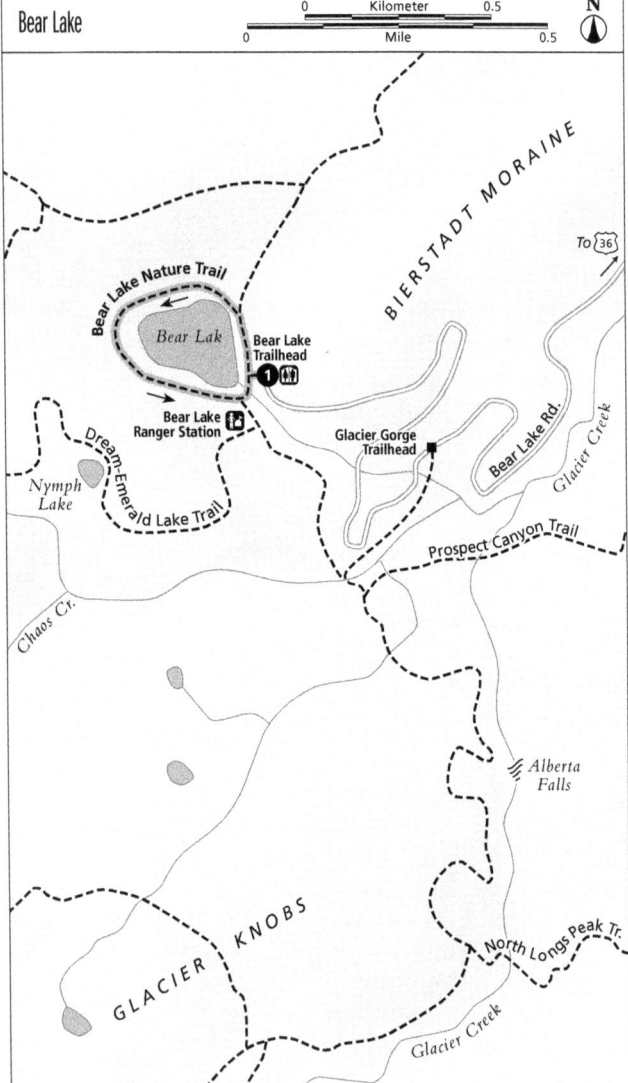

2 Nymph Lake, Dream Lake, and Emerald Lake

A gently rising trail, glacier-carved lakes, and dramatic cliffs encircling a timberline tarn as your final reward make this hike a photographer's dream and a memorable treat for all.

Start: Bear Lake Trailhead
Hiking time: 2 to 3 hours
Distance: 3.6 miles out-and-back
Difficulty: Easy to moderate
Other trail users: Human foot traffic only
Maps: Trails Illustrated #200: Rocky Mountain National Park; USGS McHenrys Peak

Highlights: Views of Hallett Peak, Flattop Mountain, and Longs Peak with pond lilies at Nymph Lake, limber pines framing Hallett and Flattop at Dream Lake, Emerald Lake
Elevations trailhead to Emerald Lake: 9,457 feet to 10,090 feet (+633 feet)

Finding the trailhead: From the Beaver Meadows Entrance Station in Estes Park, drive 0.2 mile and turn left on Bear Lake Road. Continue 9.4 miles to the parking lot and trailhead at the road's end (GPS: 40 18.7177, -105 38.7584).

The Hike

Because this trail gives hikers a great deal of spectacular scenery with relatively little effort, it is the most crowded path in Rocky Mountain National Park. Avoid crowds and see the trail at its best by starting to hike before sunrise. Starting early will provide the most dramatic light on the peaks and probably little wind. You also will meet more animals along the trail. The uphill hiking temperature will be cool. And trailhead parking is no problem when you go early!

Even by flashlight beam, signs marking the trail to Nymph and Dream Lakes are easy to follow. If you start at the ideal time, it will be too dark for photos at Nymph Lake when you arrive, but you can catch it on the way back.

On your return, use trees on the east shore to frame a photo of Hallett Peak, Flattop Mountain, and the lily pads on the lake surface. Perhaps the trees on the shore will still be in shadow and can be made a silhouette in front of the brightly lit peaks. Be sure to take your light reading off the brightest part of the picture, probably the sky.

Use the same principle to shoot Longs Peak from the trail on the north side of the lake. Just as the trail bends around Nymph's north edge, watch for upended tree roots and burned limber pine trunks, which make grand subjects for close-up abstract photos. Along the trail, the slopes above Nymph Lake are good spots for wildflower photography, as they are somewhat sheltered from wind.

At the Lake Haiyaha Trail junction, keep to the right toward Dream Lake. The lake is the ideal place to be at sunrise, when alpenglow spreads rich colors of changing hues across the faces of Hallett Peak (on the left) and Flattop Mountain. Include the dark, wind-twisted forms of limber pines or companion hikers in the foreground, below the sharp spires of Flattop. The mountain's name may seem perverse, but viewpoint is everything. From a distance, it really is flat and dull-looking. From this trail, the glacier-carved flank is the last word in drama.

Try to use divisions of light and dark within your view of Dream Lake to divide the picture vertically into thirds, and avoid making the surface of the lake a line that cuts the picture in half.

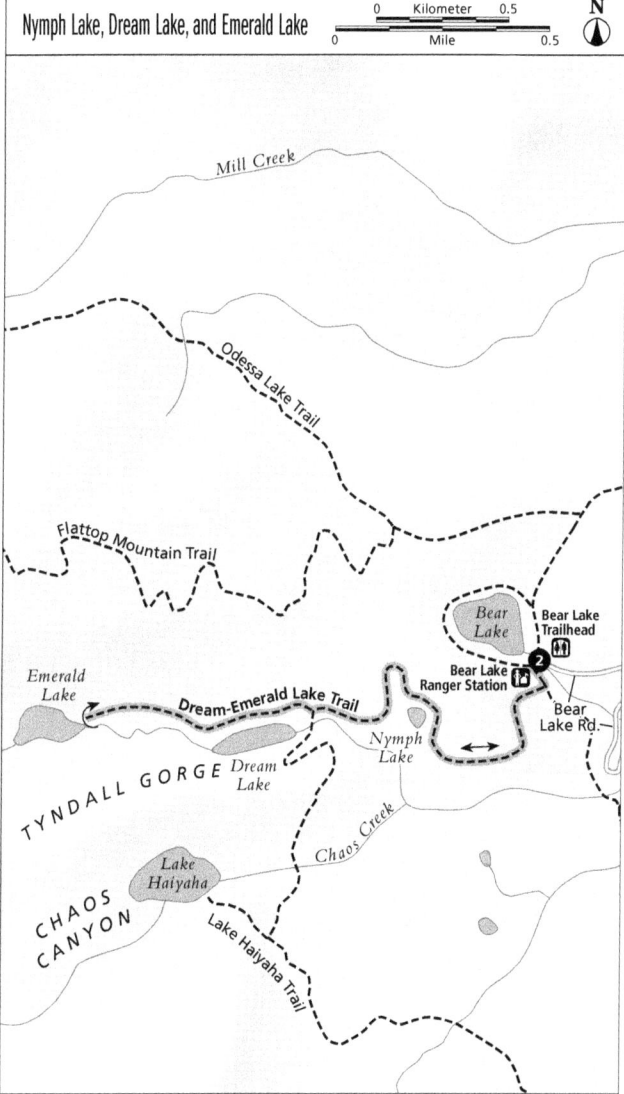

Continue to Emerald Lake. Watch for views of Tyndall Creek tumbling over bedrock accented by clumps of wildflowers below Flattop.

Miles and Directions

- **0.0** Start at the Bear Lake Trailhead by the ranger station at the west side of the parking lot. Cross a bridge to a junction for the Emerald Lake Trail. Go left on it and hike uphill through a spruce and lodgepole pine forest.
- **0.5** After gaining 255 feet of elevation, reach the south edge of Nymph Lake. Continue along its east shore with views west to Hallett Peak, then turn left along the north shore and climb below cliffs.
- **1.0** Reach a junction with the Lake Haiyaha Trail on the left. Continue straight and hike west.
- **1.1** Reach the eastern end of narrow Dream Lake and great mountain views to the west. Hike along the rocky north shore and climb west above Tyndall Creek.
- **1.8** Arrive at a rocky overlook on the east side of Emerald Lake. After enjoying the view, return back down the trail.
- **3.6** Arrive back at the trailhead.

3 Lake Haiyaha

Often crowded on the first half, much less so on the second, this trail climbs and descends to a lovely lake whose name is challenging to pronounce and worse to spell.

Start: Bear Lake Trailhead
Hiking time: 2 to 3 hours
Distance: 4 miles out-and-back
Difficulty: Easy to moderate
Other trail users: Human foot traffic only
Maps: Trails Illustrated #200: Rocky Mountain National Park; USGS McHenrys Peak

Highlights: Nymph Lake, Longs Peak/Glacier Gorge views, Lake Haiyaha
Elevations trailhead to Lake Haiyaha: 9,457 feet to 10,223 feet (+766 feet)

Finding the trailhead: From the Beaver Meadows Entrance Station in Estes Park, drive 0.2 mile and turn left on Bear Lake Road. Continue 9.4 miles to the parking lot and trailhead at the road's end (GPS: 40 18.7177, -105 38.7584).

The Hike

The first half of the hike to Lake Haiyaha follows one of the most popular (and crowded) trails in Rocky Mountain National Park. Avoid the crowds and experience the trail at its best by starting early in the day, as soon after sunrise as you can bear.

At the beginning of the hike, there are striking views of Hallett Peak above Bear Lake, seen by detouring a few yards from the Dream Lake Trail. The best views at Bear Lake probably are a short distance to the right from where you reach the shore.

The hike to Haiyaha begins on the Dream Lake Trail a short way south (left) from Bear Lake. You will see some nice views of Longs Peak and Glacier Gorge framed by aspen on the way to Nymph Lake, but even better views are at Nymph and beyond. Nymph Lake offers a perspective of Hallett Peak and Flattop Mountain different from Bear Lake's. Water lilies float on Nymph's surface.

Abstract grain patterns on burned and uprooted limber pines along the north shore are worth noting. Interesting trees around the lake frame lovely views of Thatchtop Mountain and Longs Peak. Watch for other interesting views of Longs Peak from the trail between Nymph and Dream Lakes.

The best morning scenes of the hike are at Dream Lake, which requires a short detour from the miles and directions that follow. At a trail junction, a bridge crosses Tyndall Creek; turn right before crossing the bridge and proceed to Dream Lake, where wind-shaped limber pines frame views of Hallett and Flattop.

Return to the bridge across Tyndall Creek and continue up switchbacks through a grand subalpine forest. Breaking into the open, the Lake Haiyaha Trail bends around a ridge with good views of Bear and Nymph Lakes, followed by better views of Longs Peak and Glacier Gorge.

A quarter mile before Lake Haiyaha, a connecting trail to Glacier Gorge provides access to many hiking destinations and a longer route back to Bear Lake.

Descend to cross Chaos Creek and bear right through large boulders to Lake Haiyaha, whose Native American name is said to mean "big rocks." The view of Hallett here is less exciting than from the other lakes, but a giant limber pine here is one of the most spectacular examples of this species that I have seen.

Miles and Directions

0.0 Start at the Bear Lake Trailhead by the ranger station at the west side of the parking lot. Cross a bridge to a junction for the Emerald Lake Trail. Go left on it and hike uphill through a spruce and lodgepole pine forest.

0.5 After gaining 255 feet of elevation, reach the south edge of Nymph Lake. Continue along its east shore with views west to Hallett Peak, then turn left along the north shore and climb below cliffs.

1.0 Reach a junction with the Lake Haiyaha Trail on the left. Take this trail to the lake.

2.0 Arrive at Lake Haiyaha. Return the way you came.

4.0 Arrive back at the trailhead.

4 Flattop Mountain

The hike to Flattop Mountain's summit has the most elevation gain to the highest point in this book, but views from the peak's unimpressive, flat summit are worth the effort.

Start: Bear Lake Trailhead
Hiking time: 5 to 6 hours
Difficulty: Easy to very strenuous
Distance: 8.8 miles out-and-back
Other trail users: Human foot traffic only
Maps: Trails Illustrated #200: Rocky Mountain National Park; USGS McHenrys Peak

Highlights: Dream Lake Overlook, Emerald Lake Viewpoint, summit views of Tyndall Glacier and Hallett Peak
Elevations trailhead to Flattop Mountain: 9,457 feet to 12,330 feet (+2,873 feet)

Finding the trailhead: From the Beaver Meadows Entrance Station in Estes Park, drive 0.2 mile and turn left on Bear Lake Road. Continue 9.4 miles to the parking lot and trailhead at the road's end (GPS: 40 18.7177, -105 38.7584).

The Hike

The hike to Flattop Mountain begins at Bear Lake, the busiest trailhead in Rocky Mountain National Park. After leaving the Bear Lake Loop Trail, climb the Flattop Mountain Trail into a mixed conifer forest and head west toward the Continental Divide. The high-elevation trail holds snow through late spring, so unless you are hiking in midsummer, be prepared with proper footwear, traction spikes, and trekking poles or even an ice axe for crossing mounds of snow in the forest and icy snowfields at higher elevations.

The hike offers breathtaking alpine scenery, but the summit plateau is anticlimactic with a wooden sign at a flat area pointing toward the North Inlet Trail and Tonahutu Trail on the other side of the mountain. These trails begin on Rocky Mountain National Park's west side near the town of Grand Lake and climb to the west slopes of Flattop Mountain.

From the Flattop summit, located atop the Continental Divide, enjoy views of Hallett Peak to the southeast and Longs Peak, Storm Peak, and Mount Lady Washington visible to Hallett's left. Hallett Peak is a short but difficult jaunt from Flattop Mountain, so if you have the time, the energy, and the skill to tag its summit, feel free to follow faint trails over tundra, around boulders, and across talus to the summit. This peak should only be done during ideal weather conditions. Do not attempt in rain or lightning, and allow enough time to descend during daylight.

Miles and Directions

- **0.0** From the Bear Lake Trailhead located between the ranger station and the shuttle stop at the west end of the Bear Lake Parking Lot, hike northwest over a wide footbridge and bear right toward Bear Lake, past the junction with trails to Alberta Falls and Emerald Lake Trail, to get on the Bear Lake Loop Trail. Bear right on the Bear Lake Loop Trail and hike counterclockwise around the east side of Bear Lake. The distinct angular east face of Hallett Peak appears on the skyline west-southwest of the lake, with the mellow mound of Flattop Mountain barely visible to the right of Hallett Peak.
- **0.2** Turn right onto the Bear Lake to Bierstadt Junction Trail, signed for Flattop Mountain, Fern Lake, and Odessa Lake, and hike north-northeast past the Flattop Mountain information board.
- **0.5** Turn left at the trail junction, onto the Flattop Mountain Trail, and hike west.
- **1.0** Reach the junction with the Odessa Lake / Flattop Mountain Junction Trail and bear left to stay on the Flattop Mountain Trail.

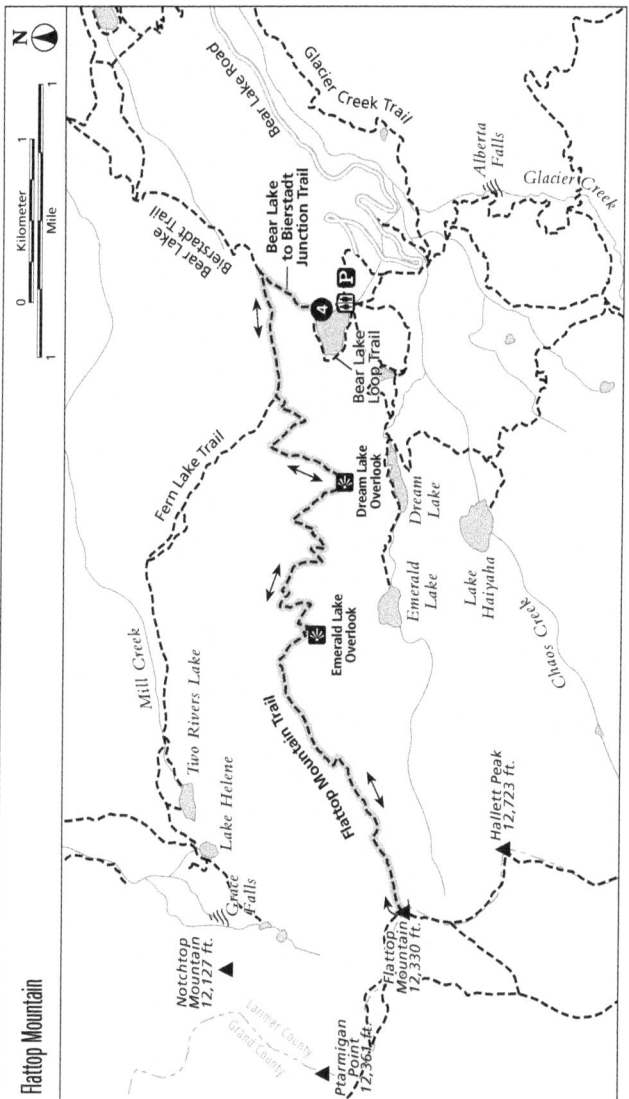

- **1.7** Continue on the trail as it climbs west, switchbacking north and south to the Dream Lake Overlook.
- **3.0** The trail continues to climb west, slowly rising out of the forest to the final switchback and the Emerald Lake Viewpoint before curving northwest to southwest across boulder-strewn tundra.
- **4.0** Reach a horse rack above Tyndall Gorge with views of Tyndall Glacier and Hallett Peak ahead and left of the trail.
- **4.4** Arrive at the summit of Flattop Mountain. Return the way you came.
- **8.8** Arrive back at the trailhead.

5 Alberta Falls

The hike to Alberta Falls follows a well-constructed path to one of the park's most photographed waterfalls.

Start: Glacier Gorge Junction Trailhead
Hiking time: 1 to 2 hours
Distance: 1.6 miles out-and-back
Difficulty: Easy
Other trail users: Equestrians
Maps: Trails Illustrated #200: Rocky Mountain National Park; USGS McHenrys Peak
Highlights: Alberta Falls
Elevations trailhead to Alberta Falls: 9,180 feet to 9,400 feet (+220 feet)

Finding the trailhead: From the Beaver Meadows Entrance Station in Estes Park, drive 0.2 mile and turn left on Bear Lake Road. Continue 8.1 miles to the parking lot and trailhead on the left (GPS: 40 18.621, -105 38.421).

The Hike

This easy path to a waterfall is one of the most popular short hikes in Rocky Mountain National Park. Along the way to Alberta Falls are many aspen that grew after a 1900 forest fire. Particularly with their fall color, these trees make this an extremely pleasant trail.

Heavy use has dictated that a certain percentage of the throngs, those who are ignorant of proper wilderness behavior, have carved their initials on the white aspen bark along this trail. Thankfully, most of this damage appears to be fairly old. The hiking public today seems to be more sophisticated about wilderness ethics, but even a tiny percentage of vandals can mess things up quite a bit.

Autumn aspens look their best when viewed from the southeast or southwest so your eyes catch the sunlight coming through the translucent leaves, creating a stained-glass-window effect. When leaves are backlit, golden color shimmers with greater intensity. With your back to the sun, you will notice duller autumn colors in all deciduous trees and bushes.

Abner Sprague, a pioneer and one of the first lodge owners in this area, named Alberta Falls for his wife. The falls plunge over a ledge gouged by glaciers. Other signs of glacial passing are boulders, gravel, light-colored clay, and bare bedrock smoothed by the moving ice. Also near the falls are now-dry potholes in the rock shaped by grinding stones carried by meltwater from retreating glaciers. This roaring torrent of ancestral Glacier Creek was much more formidable than today's stream, which still throws cooling spray on nearby hikers.

Miles and Directions

- **0.0** Begin at Glacier Gorge Junction Trailhead. Hike southwest on Glacier Gorge Trail.
- **0.3** Reach Glacier Gorge Junction. Turn left at signed junction toward Alberta Falls.
- **0.8** Arrive at Alberta Falls viewpoint. Hike back on same trail.
- **1.6** Arrive back at trailhead.

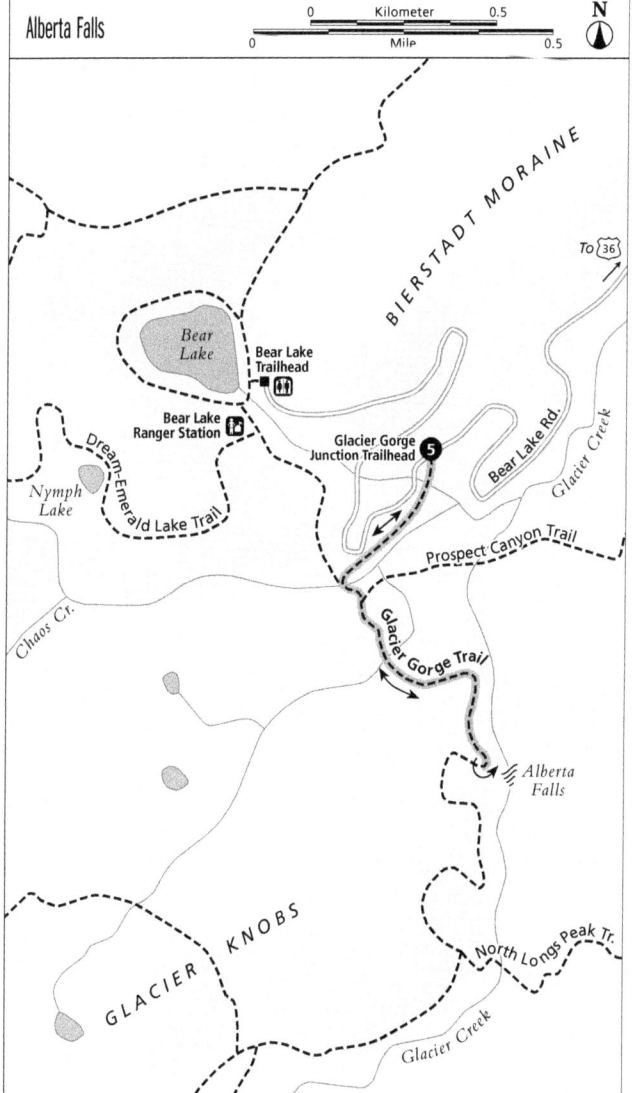

6 The Loch

By virtue of its euphonious name, Loch Vale Trail draws many hikers beyond Alberta Falls. None are disappointed by the magnificent views of cliff-bound peaks above a glacier-carved lake—The Loch.

Start: Glacier Gorge Junction Trailhead
Hiking time: 3 to 4 hours
Distance: 5.6 miles out-and-back
Difficulty: Easy to moderate
Other trail users: Equestrians as far as 3-way trail junction 2.2 miles from trailhead
Maps: Trails Illustrated #200: Rocky Mountain National Park; USGS McHenrys Peak
Highlights: Alberta Falls, The Loch
Elevations trailhead to the Loch: 9,180 feet to 10,200 feet (+1,020 feet)

Finding the trailhead: From the Beaver Meadows Entrance Station in Estes Park, drive 0.2 mile and turn left on Bear Lake Road. Continue 8.1 miles to the parking lot and trailhead on the left (GPS: 40 18.621, -105 38.421).

The Hike

Estes Park pioneer Abner Sprague used a pun to name The Loch and Loch Vale, the valley in which this photogenic lake sits. He named these features for a guest at his lodge, a banker named Locke. Sprague changed the spelling to *loch,* the Scottish word for lake, a clever joke that causes some confusion a century later. But many people who judge this to be the prettiest lake in Rocky Mountain National Park think calling it The Lake is appropriate.

Named for Sprague's wife, Alberta Falls may be the most-photographed falls in the park. Beyond the falls the trail climbs amid rocks through land slowly recovering from a 1900 forest fire. Watch for colorful wildflowers growing against burned, weathered wood.

In the rock fields where the trail levels then descends slightly, marmots and pikas may whistle and chirp at passing hikers but likely will not permit close approach.

In a forested bowl missed by the 1900 fire, the trail splits three ways. A sign indicates the middle way goes to The Loch. Beyond the junction, Icy Brook tumbles with a view of Taylor Peak above.

Taylor Glacier, nearby snowfields, and the Cathedral Wall dominate views from The Loch. Twisted limber pines on the rocky shore create a dramatic foreground.

Miles and Directions

- **0.0** Begin at Glacier Gorge Junction Trailhead. Hike southwest on Glacier Gorge Trail.
- **0.3** Reach junction with trail from Bear Lake. Go straight and turn left at next junction toward Alberta Falls.
- **0.8** Arrive at Alberta Falls. Continue south on trail.
- **1.6** Reach junction with North Longs Peak Trail on left. Go straight on Glacier Gorge Trail.
- **2.1** Reach junction with Loch Vale Trail. Go right up Loch Vale.
- **2.8** Arrive at The Loch. Hike around right (north) side of lake and follow Icy Brook. Return the way you came.
- **5.6** Arrive back at trailhead.

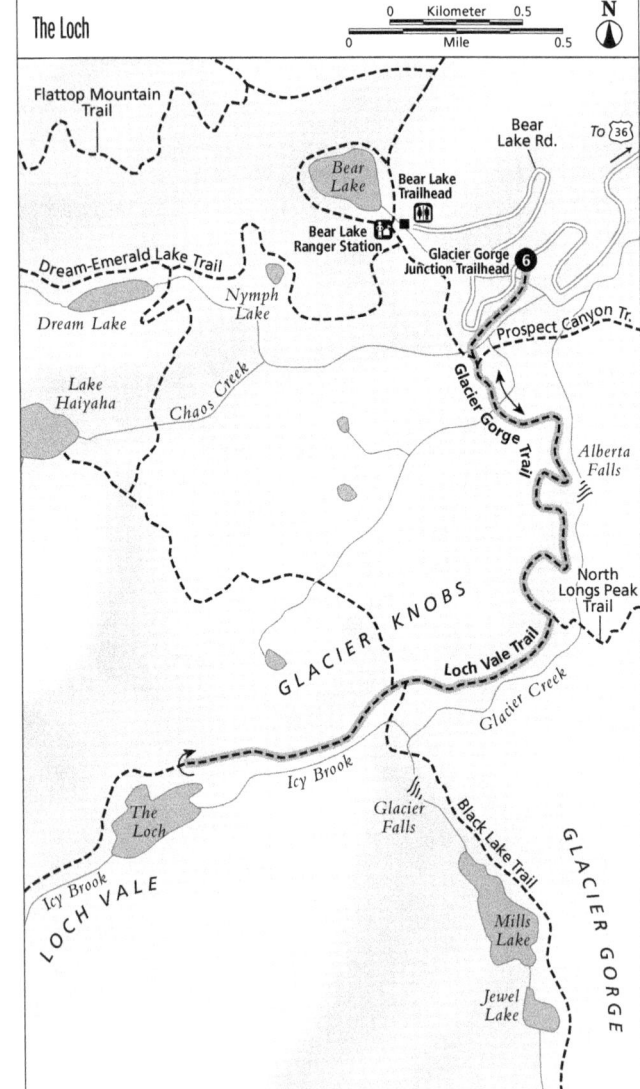

7 Mills Lake

This very popular hike leads to a rock-rimmed lake situated dramatically below Longs Peak and the extremely jagged Keyboard of the Winds.

Start: Glacier Gorge Junction Trailhead
Hiking time: 3 to 4 hours
Distance: 5 miles out-and-back
Difficulty: Easy to moderate
Other trail users: Equestrians as far as a three-way trail junction 2.2 miles from the trailhead

Maps: Trails Illustrated #200: Rocky Mountain National Park; USGS McHenrys Peak
Highlights: Alberta Falls, Mills Lake
Elevations trailhead to Mills Lake: 9,180 feet to 9,960 feet (+780 feet)

Finding the trailhead: From the Beaver Meadows Entrance Station in Estes Park, drive 0.2 mile and turn left on Bear Lake Road. Continue 8.1 miles to the parking lot and trailhead on the left (GPS: 40 18.621, -105 38.421).

The Hike

Mills Lake is named for Enos Mills, the father of Rocky Mountain National Park. Mills wrote many articles and books (most still in print) and gave many lectures urging the establishment of a national park around Longs Peak. Six years of concentrated effort resulted in the park's creation in 1915.

Many hikers consider Mills Lake the prettiest lake in the park, a bold claim where there are so many outstanding contenders for this praise (see previous hike, "The Loch"). Without doubt, this popular destination is extremely lovely in its dramatic setting below Longs Peak.

Along the first mile of the trail, Glacier Creek is exciting, especially where it shoots over Alberta Falls. Also along the first part of the trail, notice the weather-etched patterns in the grain of red, gray, and black wood killed in a 1900 forest fire.

Scrambling over glacier-scoured bedrock in Glacier Gorge, you will see several spectacular views of Longs Peak, tallest in the park, and the jagged Keyboard of the Winds. The round boulders left isolated on the bedrock by melting glaciers and the twisted shapes of limber pines increase the interest of this scene.

Unlike most lakes on the east side of the national park, Mills Lake is prettiest in the late afternoon. This fact alone is enough to merit praise from hikers who are tired of rising before dawn to see the best light on the peaks. Afternoon skies frequently contain clouds, which can either add interesting shapes to an empty sky or throw the entire landscape into muted shadow.

Miles and Directions

- **0.0** Begin at the Glacier Gorge Junction Trailhead. Hike southwest on the Glacier Gorge Trail.
- **0.3** Reach Glacier Gorge Junction and turn left. Hike uphill past Alberta Falls to a ridgetop east of the twin Glacier Knobs.
- **1.6** Reach a junction with North Longs Peak Trail on the left. Bend right on Glacier Gorge Trail and hike west across a slope above Glacier Creek.
- **2.1** Reach a junction with signed Loch Vale Trail. Go left on Black Lake Trail toward Mills Lake and cross a bridge over the creek. Climb south, passing Glacier Falls to the west.
- **2.5** Arrive at Mills Lake. Return the way you came.
- **5.0** Arrive back at the trailhead.

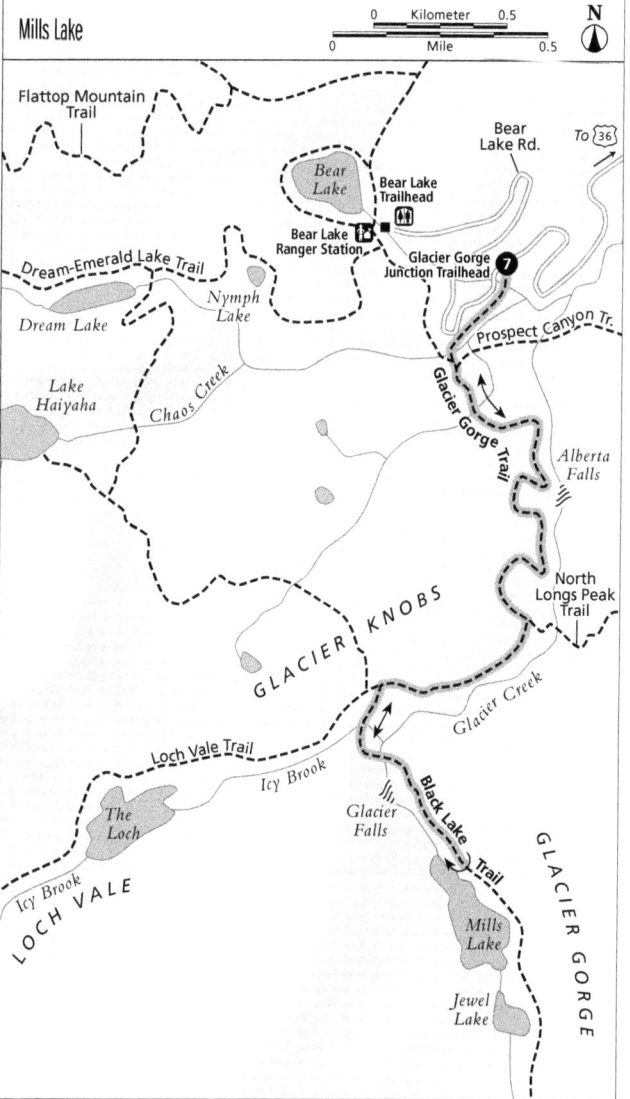

8 Bierstadt Lake

Though small, the Bierstadt Lake Trailhead parking area doesn't fill as quickly as other parking lots on Bear Lake Road, making this hike a good option during the busiest times of day.

Start: Bierstadt Lake Trailhead
Hiking time: 2 to 3 hours
Difficulty: Easy
Distance: 3.7-mile lollipop loop
Other trail users: Equestrians
Maps: Trails Illustrated #200: Rocky Mountain National Park; USGS McHenrys Peak and Longs Peak

Highlights: Views of Longs Peak from Bierstadt Lake, aspen along south side of Bierstadt Moraine
Elevations trailhead to Bierstadt Lake: 8,850 feet to 9,440 feet (+590 feet)

Finding the trailhead: From the Beaver Meadows Entrance Station in Estes Park, drive 0.2 mile and turn left on Bear Lake Road. Continue 6.8 miles to the parking lot and trailhead on the right (GPS: 40 19.230, -105 37.423).

The Hike

Bierstadt Lake's formation may be unique among the lakes of Rocky Mountain National Park: It rests in a basin formed by the merging of two lateral moraines, rock ridges dumped by glaciers as they flowed down mountain valleys.

Most of the park's lakes were made by glaciers, but in ways that set them beneath scenic peaks. Bierstadt just sits in the midst of woods, although the view across from the north shore toward Longs Peak in the distance is not bad. It seems ironic that comparatively mundane Bierstadt Lake was named for a nineteenth-century painter whose Rocky Mountain scenes were very grandiose.

Bierstadt Lake

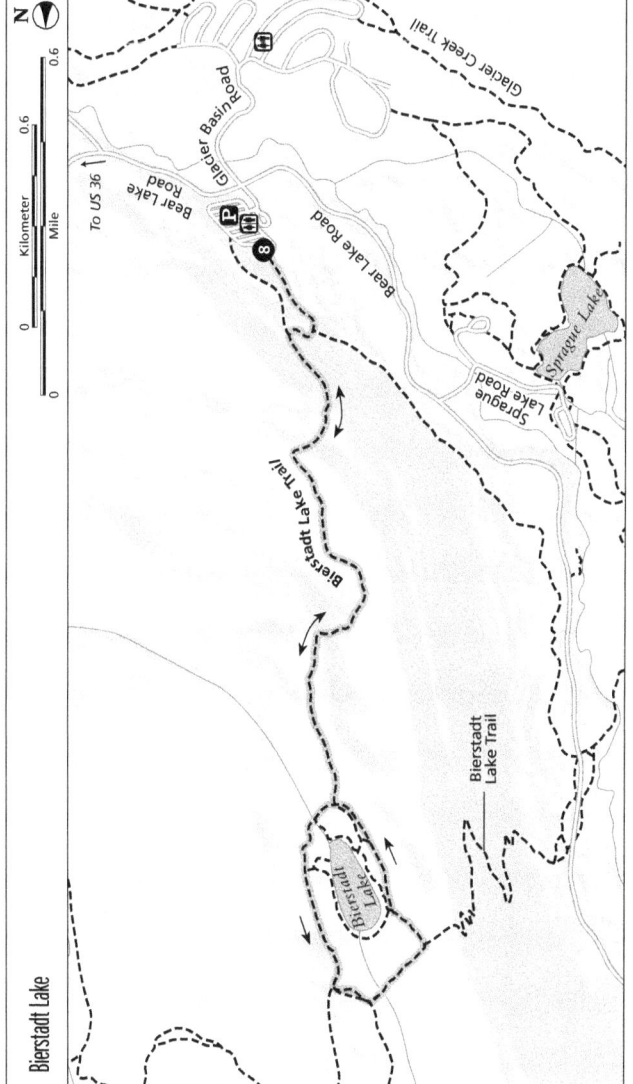

Bierstadt Lake Trail switchbacks through open lodgepole pine and aspen woods that grew up after a 1900 forest fire. Nice at any time of year, this trail is magic in autumn when aspen leaves have turned golden. Mountains in the distance form interesting silhouettes, dark and brooding backgrounds that make the leaves stand out all the more brilliantly.

The area around Bierstadt Lake is a maze of trails, but signs provide adequate guidance. One trail circles the lake, another descends to Hollowell Park, and a third heads down to the Bear Lake Shuttle parking area. After circling the lake, take care to choose the same path you ascended, which descends to the Bierstadt Lake Trailhead.

Miles and Directions

- **0.0** From the Bierstadt Lake Trailhead, hike north on switchbacks, past Bierstadt Moraine, on left.
- **1.4** Arrive at south end of Bierstadt Lake. Turn right and hike counterclockwise, making your way to the lake's edge. Continue on the trail around the lake.
- **2.3** Reach the end of the loop and turn right to descend the trail.
- **3.7** Arrive at Bierstadt Lake Trailhead.

9 Sprague Lake

The loop trail around Sprague Lake is nearly flat and very easy to walk. It provides many photography opportunities of the Front Range, especially in the early morning.

Start: Sprague Lake Parking Area
Hiking time: 30 minutes to 1 hour
Distance: 0.8-mile lollipop loop
Difficulty: Very easy
Other trail users: Wheelchairs, strollers
Maps: Trails Illustrated #200: Rocky Mountain National Park; USGS Longs Peak
Highlights: Views of Front Range, beaver ponds
Elevations trailhead to Sprague Lake: 8,690 feet to 8,688 feet (–2 feet)

Finding the trailhead: From the Beaver Meadows Entrance Station in Estes Park, drive 0.2 mile and turn left on Bear Lake Road. Continue 5.7 miles and turn left on Sprague Lake Road, then drive 0.3 mile to the parking lot and trailhead (GPS: 40 19.2268, -105 36.4716).

The Hike

Gray jays, Steller's jays, and sometimes Clark's nutcrackers hang around the picnic area at the Sprague Lake parking lot, waiting to steal unguarded morsels. Try to photograph these birds in the low branches that serve as their lookout points, which gives a much nicer background than a picnic bench or the scantily vegetated ground.

Mallard ducks here are very tame and easy to photograph. Try for some action instead of the typical static pose: stretching a wing, interacting with other ducks, swimming among attractive shoreline grasses. In the spring you can often photograph cute baby mallards at Sprague Lake. Try using them also as silhouettes in the foreground of pictures of the Front Range from the east side of the lake.

Walking around the lake provides at least two good perspectives of Otis Peak, Hallett Peak, and Flattop Mountain in the Front Range. The chances for reflections of the mountains on a still lake surface are excellent early in the day. The first good spot, if you begin walking left on the north side, is in a sheltered cove where a stream exits the 13-acre lake. Pines form a dark-shadowed frame for the mountains, the silhouetted needles filling empty sky with interesting shapes and directing the eye to the mountains.

Also here is one of the most photogenic blue spruces in the area. This single example of Colorado's state tree presents a classic cone shape when viewed from the east, across the water, and stands out nicely from the surrounding lodgepole pines.

The second good viewpoint of the Front Range is at the east end of the lake at its second outlet. There are few trees here to serve as good foreground for pictures of the mountains, but you can use bushes or flowers along the shore for this purpose. Rounded boulders that were deposited by a melting glacier sit in the water near the shore. The round shapes of these granite rocks make an interesting foreground element to add depth to your photo.

Miles and Directions

- **0.0** Start at the Sprague Lake Trailhead at the southeast corner of the parking lot. Hike east across a bridge and after about 250 feet, reach a junction at the start of the lake loop. Go left.
- **0.2** Reach a junction. Keep left on the main trail or go right and walk a short path along the northern lakeshore.

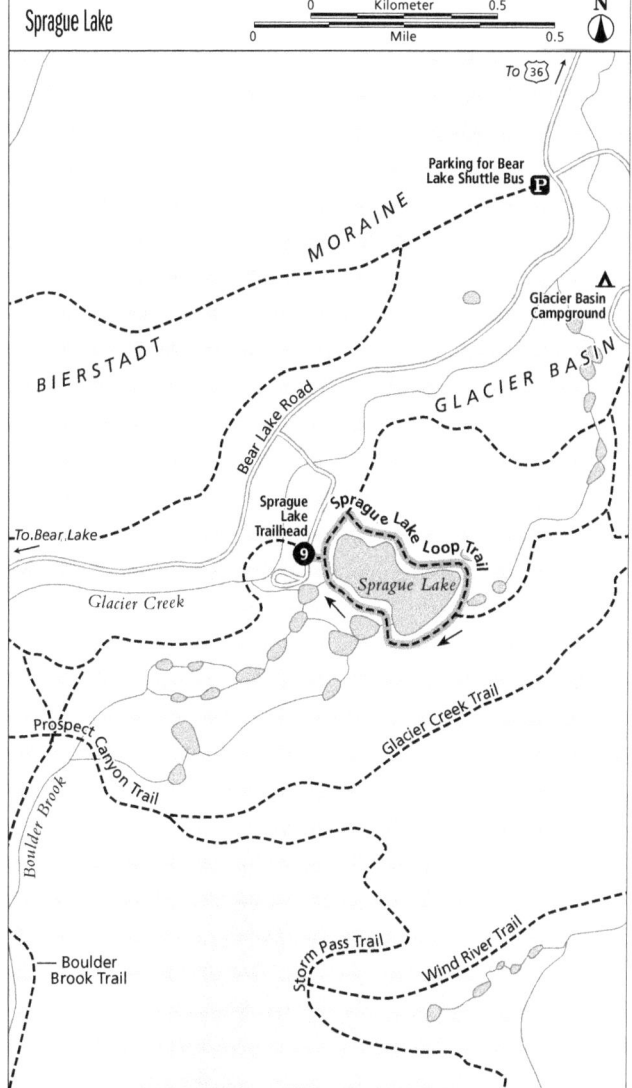

0.25 Reach a junction with the lakeshore spur. Continue straight on the main trail around the lake.
0.75 Return to the first Y-junction and turn left.
0.8 Arrive back at the trailhead.

10 Cub Lake

The Cub Lake Trail meanders across a meadow recovering well from wildfire damage, then it climbs through burned forest to the lake, still displaying yellow pond lilies.

Start: Cub Lake Trailhead
Distance: 4.6 miles out-and-back
Hiking time: About 3 hours
Difficulty: Easy to moderate
Other trail users: Equestrians
Maps: Trails Illustrated #200: Rocky Mountain National Park; USGS McHenrys Peak and Longs Peak
Highlights: Wildflowers, wildlife, Cub Lake
Elevations trailhead to Cub Lake: 8,080 feet to 8,620 feet (+540 feet)

Finding the trailhead: From the Beaver Meadows Entrance Station in Estes Park, drive 0.2 mile and turn left on Bear Lake Road. Drive 1.2 miles and turn right toward Moraine Park Campground. Drive 0.5 mile and turn left on Fern Lake Road. Continue 1.5 miles to the parking lot and trailhead (GPS: 40 21.2897, -105 37.8688).

The Hike

From the trailhead, hike south on the Cub Lake Trail, among the richest in the park for the wildflowers and wildlife seen along its length. Turkeys, moose, and bats have been spotted along the trails and around the ponds. For much of its route across the level floor of Moraine Park, the trail is extremely easy to walk. Spoiled by the initial easiness of the trail, hikers may think the last 0.5 mile is rather steep.

Jammed with innumerable opportunities for close-up photos, the Cub Lake Trail is not notable for its scenery, compared with much of the rest of the park. Low scenery potential and extensive opportunities for studying the small, intimate details that are abundant along the way to Cub

Lake make this an ideal trail for cloudy-day hiking. Insect repellent may be beneficial.

A December 2012 wildfire actually improved much wildflower habitat by opening former forest to sunlight. The wetlands through which the trail initially passes are recovering as new growth rises from the roots of burned water birch. Rare wood lilies, their bulbs hidden beneath the ground, also emerged again to display their spotted orange grandeur.

The best view is looking westerly toward Stones Peak from the northeast end of the lake, which is reached after 2.3 miles. Although the 2012 forest fire did nothing to help the vista, the vegetation growing back exemplifies plant succession after a fire or other disturbance. The water lilies on the lake's surface denote the gradual filling in of Cub Lake. Baby mallards among the lily pads are delightful; the lake's leeches (which don't prey on humans) are less lovely.

Miles and Directions

- **0.0** Start at the Cub Lake Trailhead. Hike south for 260 feet, cross a footbridge over the Big Thompson River, and continue south on the west side of Moraine Park through meadows and wetlands.
- **0.5** Reach a junction on the left with South Lateral Moraine Trail at the southwest corner of Moraine Park. Keep on the main trail and hike west up a glaciated valley.
- **0.8** Cross a rock outcrop and pass beaver ponds to the left. Look for moose in the ponds.
- **1.4** Reach the valley's end below a cliff and hike west up pine-covered slopes.
- **1.5** Pass more beaver ponds in an upper valley and continue uphill.
- **2.3** Arrive at the northeast side of Cub Lake and the best mountain views. After admiring the vista, turn around and return the way you came.
- **4.6** Arrive back at the trailhead.

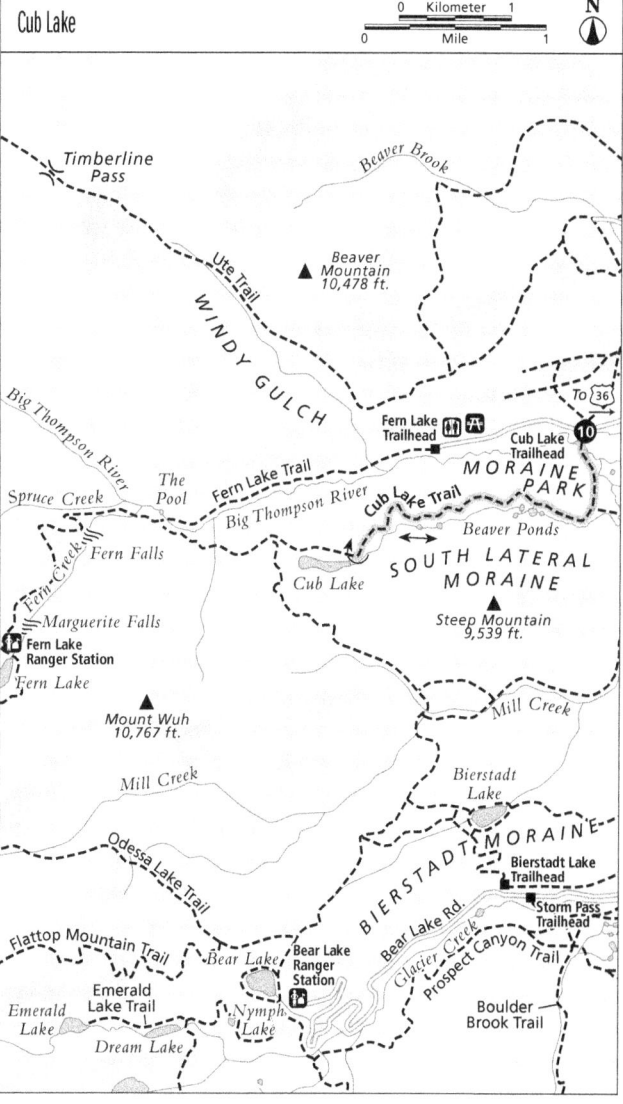

11 Fern Lake

The Fern Lake Trail follows white water on an easy grade along the Big Thompson River to a quiet spot below a timber bridge buttressed by granite outcrops before continuing to the less-popular, but also less-crowded, Fern Lake.

Start: Fern Lake Trailhead
Hiking time: 5 to 6 hours
Distance: 7.6 miles out-and-back
Difficulty: Easy to moderate
Other trail users: Equestrians
Maps: Trails Illustrated #200: Rocky Mountain National Park; USGS McHenrys Peak
Highlights: Arch Rocks, The Pool, Fern Falls
Elevations trailhead to Fern Lake: 8,165 feet to 9,503 feet (+1,338 feet)

Finding the trailhead: From the Beaver Meadows Entrance Station in Estes Park, drive 0.2 mile and turn left (south) on Bear Lake Road. Drive 1.2 miles and turn right toward Moraine Park Campground. Drive 0.5 mile and turn left on Fern Lake Road. Continue 2.2 miles to the parking lot and trailhead (GPS: 40 21.2897, -105 37.8688).

The Hike

Bracken ferns grow along the Big Thompson River to the first stop on this hike, The Pool. These ferns grow in stream valleys, where moisture is readily available. Look closely at the lacy patterns of the fern leaves, which are particularly lovely in fall when they turn a rusty golden color.

The Fern Lake Trail often emerges from the forest into meadows opened by beavers removing aspen. Throughout the warm months, these meadows produce many wildflowers that brighten the open spots with masses of color.

Many huge rocks border the trail, some carried to their resting places within the ice of glaciers flowing from the Continental Divide, occasionally visible ahead. Even more boulders, those not rounded by grinding ice, fell to their present spots after the ice melted. Rocky debris fans down the slopes, some of the older rockfalls mellowed by invading trees and shrubs. A rockfall from July 2013 is easy to see where the trail passes between towering megaliths called Arch Rocks.

Visible from the trail is the slope across the river burned by a 2012 forest fire. In one spot, as the trail approaches The Pool, the fire jumped the river and burned trees through which the trail passes. Many other dead trees line the trail, not killed by fire but by mountain pine beetles, stockpiling fuel for future conflagrations.

The Pool is a wide spot where a bridge crosses the Big Thompson River, providing a sturdy platform for viewing swirling patterns of white water. Rock ledges at water's edge here often are nest sites for water ouzels (American dippers), entertaining gray birds that live entirely within spray distance of water. An ouzel enters its moss-domed nest through a hole in the nest's side. You may find an inconspicuous nest by watching a bird repeatedly fly back and forth to the same spot along the stream.

Miles and Directions

- **0.0** Start at the Fern Lake Trailhead and hike west on the north bank of the Big Thompson River.
- **1.7** Cross the river on a footbridge and reach a junction on the left with Cub Lake Trail. Continue straight past The Pool on the right.
- **1.9** Cross a bridge over Fern Creek.
- **2.6** Reach Fern Falls. Continue south up the trail.

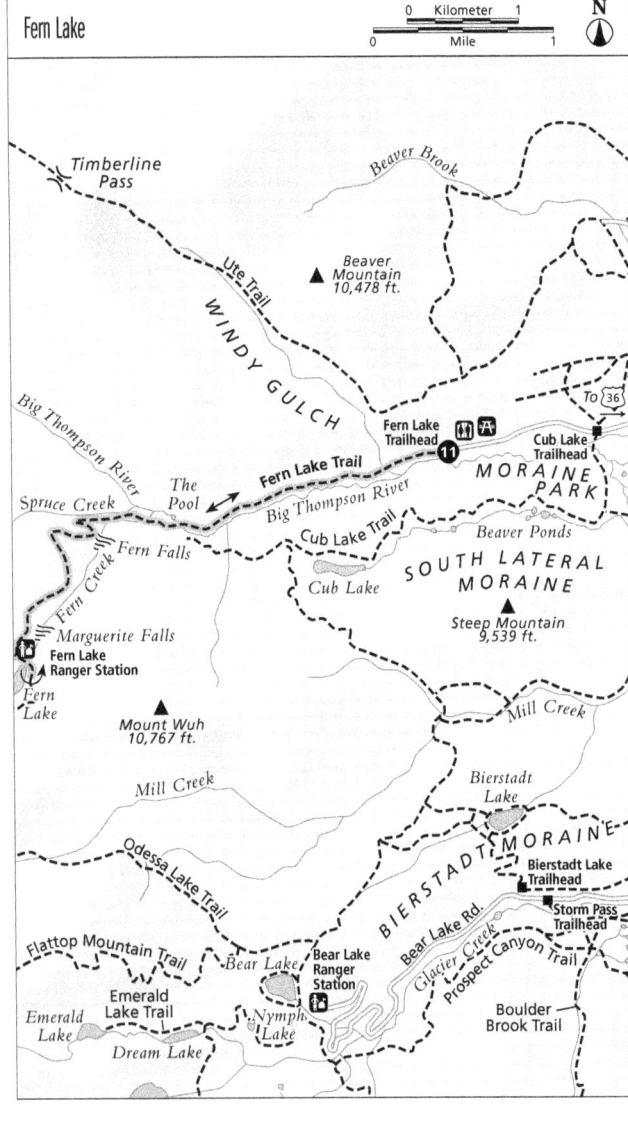

3.7 Reach a junction on the right with Spruce Lake Trail. Continue straight to Fern Lake.
3.8 Reach the north shore of Fern Lake and admire the view. Return the way you came.
7.6 Arrive back at the trailhead.

12 Spruce Lake

Perfect for the solitude-seeking hiker, this lesser-known diversion from the Fern Lake Trail on the Spruce Lake Trail leads to a spruce-ringed tarn reflecting statuesque Castle Rock.

Start: Fern Lake Trailhead
Hiking time: 6 to 7 hours
Distance: 9 miles out-and-back
Difficulty: Easy to strenuous
Other trail users: Equestrians
Maps: Trails Illustrated #200: Rocky Mountain National Park; USGS McHenrys Peak

Highlights: Arch Rocks, The Pool, Fern Falls
Elevations trailhead to Spruce Lake: 8,165 feet to 9,680 feet (+1,515 feet)

Finding the trailhead: From the Beaver Meadows Entrance Station in Estes Park, drive 0.2 mile and turn left (south) on Bear Lake Road. Drive 1.2 miles and turn right toward Moraine Park Campground. Drive 0.5 mile and turn left on Fern Lake Road. Continue 2.2 miles to the parking lot and trailhead (GPS: 40 21.2897, -105 37.8688).

The Hike

These trails offer dramatic alpine scenery, a waterfall, golden aspens in autumn, plentiful wildlife, and a lovely lake. Gaining over 1,500 feet from trailhead to Spruce Lake, the hike may prove challenging for some hikers. Find your comfortable pace, and take breaks to snack and hydrate.

Expect to see many hikers along the trail to the Pool, fewer past The Pool toward Fern Lake, and still fewer past the Spruce Lake junction. Enjoy this rare, peaceful treat in Rocky Mountain National Park.

Spruce Lake

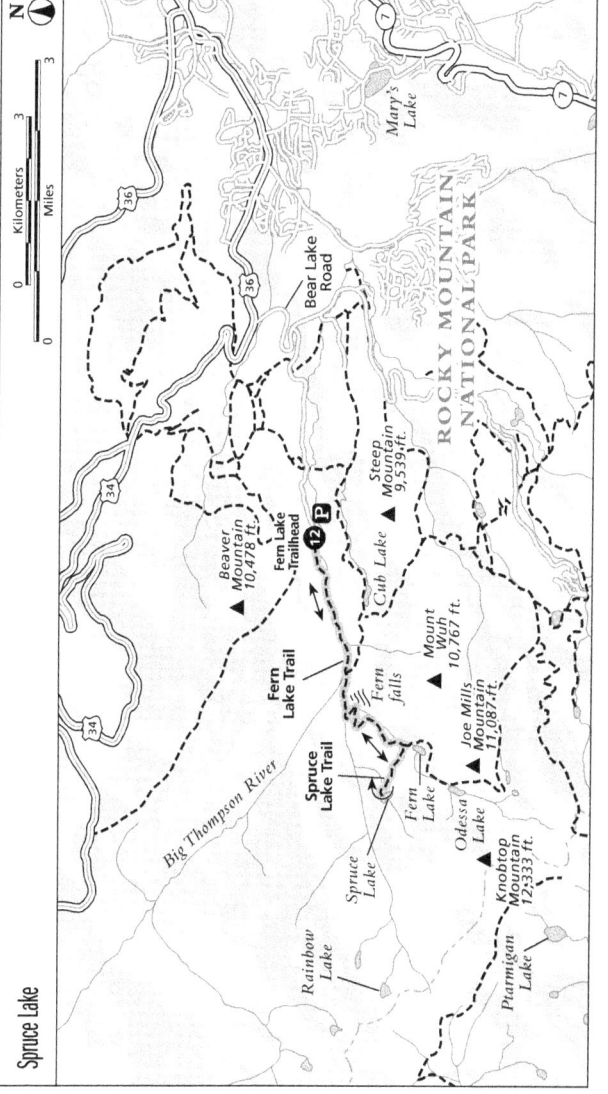

Miles and Directions

0.0 Start at the Fern Lake Trailhead and hike west on the north bank of the Big Thompson River.

1.7 Cross the river on a footbridge and reach a junction on the left with Cub Lake Trail. Continue straight past The Pool on the right.

1.9 Cross a bridge over Fern Creek.

2.6 Reach Fern Falls. Continue south up the trail.

3.7 Reach a junction and turn right onto Spruce Lake Trail. Continue for 0.8 mile.

4.5 Arrive at Spruce Lake. Return the way you came.

9.0 Arrive back at the trailhead.

Fall River Entrance and East Side of Trail Ridge Road (Estes Park)

13 Chipmunk Lake and Ypsilon Lake

Pause by Chipmunk Lake and then continue to Ypsilon Lake, a remote tarn in the Mummy Range hidden in a rugged cirque below Ypsilon Mountain and the twin Spectacle Lakes.

Start: Lawn Lake Trailhead
Hiking time: 6 to 7 hours
Distance: 9 miles out-and-back
Difficulty: Easy to very strenuous
Other trail users: Equestrians
Maps: Trails Illustrated #200: Rocky Mountain National Park; USGS Trail Ridge
Highlights: Ypsilon Falls
Elevations trailhead to Ypsilon Lake: 8,540 feet to 10,550 feet (+2,010 feet)

Finding the trailhead: From the Fall River Entrance Station in Estes Park, drive 2.1 miles and turn right on Old Fall River Road. Continue 0.1 mile to the parking lot and trailhead on the right (GPS: 40 24.4327, -105 37.5704).

The Hike

Granite cliffs, talus slopes, and pockets of spruce surround clear Ypsilon Lake, a glacial tarn tucked into a cirque on the south flank of the Mummy Range. The lake lies below the abrupt, southeastern face of Ypsilon Mountain, the fifth-highest peak in Rocky Mountain National Park, although the mountain with its distinctive Y-shaped gullies is unseen from the lake. In a higher cirque below the rocky peak are the Spectacle Lakes, two dramatic lakes reached by a steep, unofficial path that scrambles up bedrock and talus.

The Ypsilon Lake Trail, listed on the National Register of Historic Places, climbs steadily up a blunt ridge from its junction with the Lawn Lake Trail. Besides the lovely lake at trail's end, the path swings past spruce-fringed Chipmunk Lake and wilderness campsites. Just beyond the lake is noisy "Ypsilon Falls," a two-tiered waterfall that fills a plunge pool, then squeezes through a granite gap to Ypsilon Lake.

The Ypsilon Lake Trail, built between 1907 and 1912, predates the establishment of the national park and was included on tourist maps as early as 1915. Early mountaineer Frederick Chapin and his wife, Alice, named the mountain in 1887. Chapin recalled that the pair, lounging in a meadow, saw a "great peak with a steep wall facing the east. . . . A large snowfield lay on the eastern face, two flittering bands of ice extended skyward to the ridge of the mountain, forming a perfect Y. My wife said to me, 'Its name shall be Ypsilon Peak.'"

Miles and Directions

0.0 Begin at the Lawn Lake Trailhead. Hike north on the Lawn Lake Trail, and after 0.1 mile, bear left at a trail junction and stay on the trail. Follow the trail north above a gorge carved by the Lawn Lake flood.

1.5 Reach a junction with Ypsilon Lake Trail. Go left on it, cross a footbridge over Roaring River, and then ascend timber steps. The trail climbs steadily northwest through forest on a blunt ridge with limited views.

4.0 Reach Chipmunk Lake on the right. Continue past backcountry campsites.

4.5 Arrive at Ypsilon Lake's wooded southern shore. To see Ypsilon Falls, continue around the west side of the lake for 0.1 mile to the waterfall. From the lake, return the way you came.

9.0 Arrive back at the trailhead.

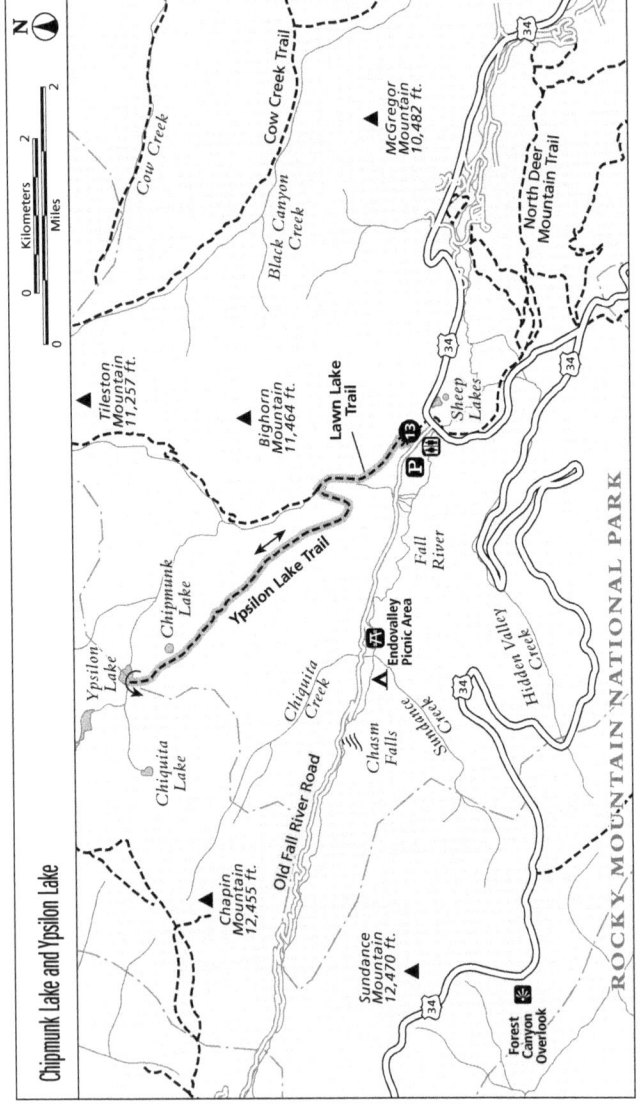

14 Horseshoe Falls

The Roaring River tumbles south toward Horseshoe Park from Crystal Lake, providing a chaotic, stepped spectacle of fan, veil, horsetail, and slide falls that make up Horseshoe Falls.

Start: West Alluvial Fan Trailhead
Hiking time: 15 to 30 minutes
Distance: 0.4 mile out-and-back
Difficulty: Very easy
Other trail users: Wheelchairs, strollers
Maps: Trails Illustrated #200: Rocky Mountain National Park; USGS Trail Ridge
Highlights: Interpretive signs, Horseshoe Falls
Elevations trailhead to Horseshoe Falls: 8,550 feet to 8,680 feet (+130 feet)

Finding the trailhead: From the Fall River Entrance Station in Estes Park, drive 2.1 miles and turn right on Old Fall River Road. Continue 0.8 mile to the parking lot and trailhead on the right (GPS: 40 24.645, -105 38.251).

The Hike

Horseshoe Falls, a cascade over granite bedrock, and the Alluvial Fan, a delta of rocks and gravel on the north edge of Horseshoe Park, illustrate the explosive force of raw nature. On July 15, 1982, an earthen dam at Lawn Lake failed, sending a surge of 29 million gallons of water, huge boulders, and toppled trees for 4 miles down the Roaring River. Two campers died at Aspenglen Campground, and Estes Park was flooded. After the water slowed, a 42-acre alluvial fan spread boulders and gravel up to 44 feet deep in Horseshoe Park.

Horseshoe Falls is reached by paved Alluvial Fan Trail, which connects the West and East Alluvial Fan Trailheads

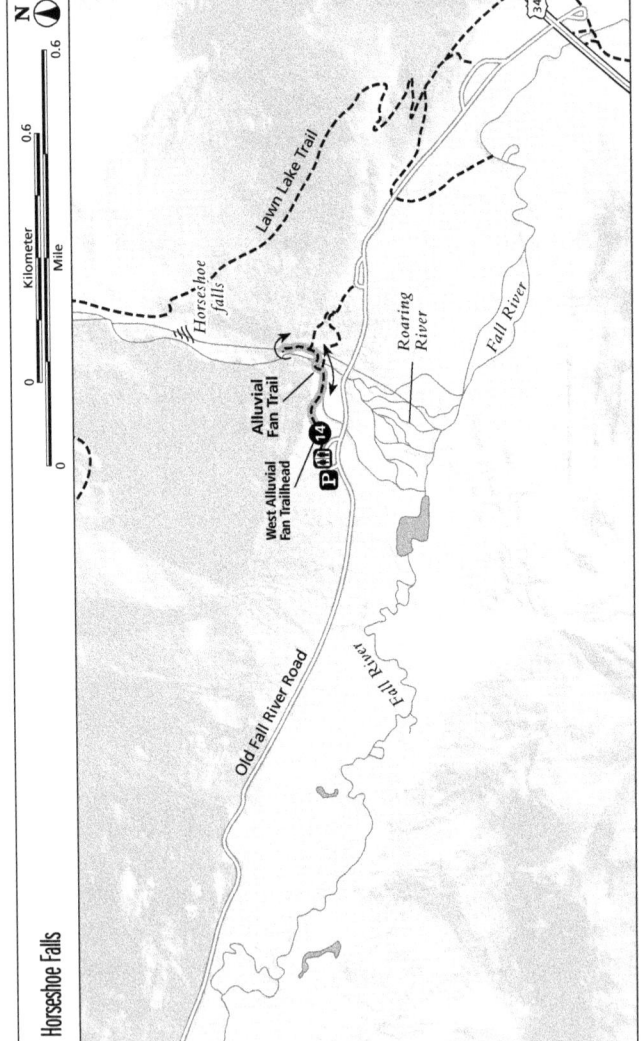

and parking lots. The waterfall is visible from the road and trail. Interpretive signs scatter along the path, including one detailing the Lawn Lake Flood.

Miles and Directions

- **0.0** Begin at West Alluvial Fan Trailhead at west parking lot. Follow trail northeast, cross a bridge, and hike to waterfall viewpoint on paved trail.
- **0.2** For more adventure, scramble north to base of falls. Return the way you came.
- **0.4** Arrive back at trailhead.

15 Chasm Falls

Tucked into a roadside gorge, the Fall River pours down a dramatic chute waterfall at Chasm Falls.

Start: Endovalley Picnic Area
Hiking time: 2 to 3 hours
Distance: 2.6 miles out-and-back
Difficulty: Easy
Other trail users: Equestrians
Maps: Trails Illustrated #200: Rocky Mountain National Park; USGS Trail Ridge
Highlights: Wildlife, Chasm Falls
Elevations trailhead to Chasm Falls: 8,640 feet to 9,000 feet (+360 feet)

Finding the trailhead: From the Fall River Entrance Station in Estes Park, drive 2.1 miles and turn right on Old Fall River Road. Continue 1.8 miles to the parking lot and trailhead on the left (GPS: 40 24.816, -105 39.473).

The Hike

Old Fall River Road was the first motorized route to transect Rocky Mountain National Park, opening in 1920. Many centuries earlier, however, Arapaho travelers called this the Dog Trail because their dogs pulled travois bearing the Native Americans' burdens over this route to the other side of the mountains.

This is one of the park's best areas to see elk, as indicated by the heavy black scarring of aspen trunks along the paved road that runs along the Fall River valley floor. Elk strip off the bark for winter food. The unpaved road is closed to vehicles in winter, but can be hiked year-round. However, for a winter hike, the road is closed to vehicles farther down, so you would have to start your hike at the

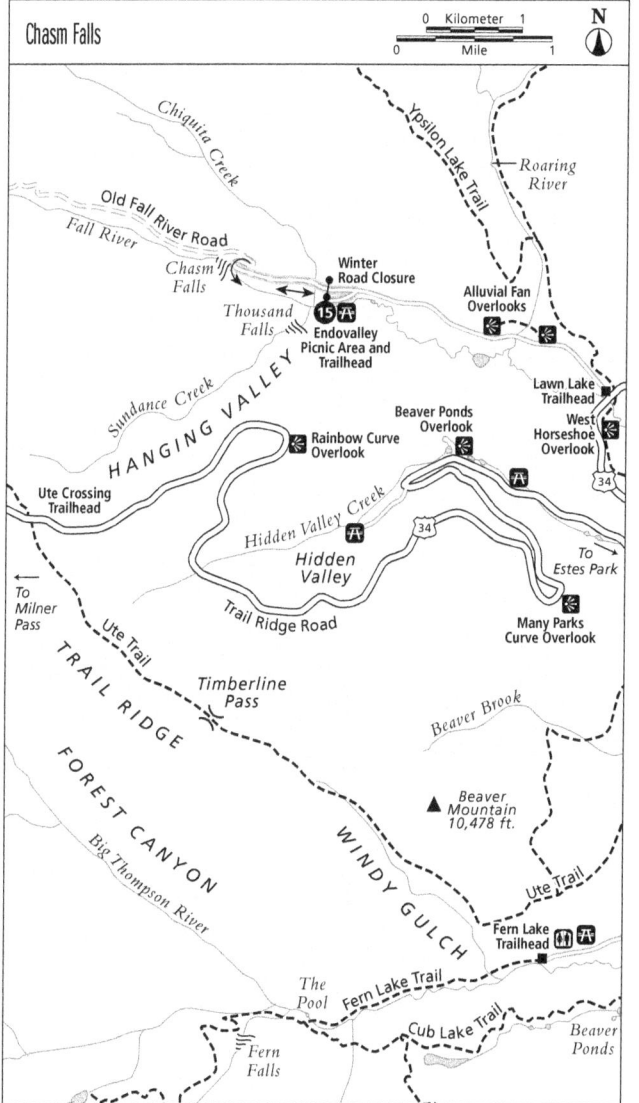

West Alluvial Trailhead. This makes for a slightly longer hike, at 4.8 miles out and back. When the road is open, you can drive to the falls, but this pleasant 2.6-mile hike will make you appreciate the lovely waterfall even more.

Potholes at the base of Chasm Falls were scoured thousands of years ago by glacial meltwater dropping through ice cracks and swirling rocks. Fall River continues the same process at the base of the 25-foot falls. Be very careful of steep, slick surfaces when you are near the falls.

Hikers along Old Fall River Road may notice results of September 2013 flooding, which wiped out sections of the road. This damage closed the road for repair during 2014. If you extend your hike beyond Chasm Falls, watch for bighorn sheep on rock outcrops north of the road. Elk often appear on the road itself and across the valley on the side of Sundance Mountain.

Miles and Directions

- **0.0** From the Endovalley Picnic area, walk to Old Fall River Road and hike up (westward) the unpaved road.
- **1.3** Arrive at Chasm Falls, located below the road. Descend a short trail for close-up views. Return the way you came.
- **2.6** Arrive back at the Endovalley Picnic Area.

16 Roger Toll Memorial

A short, paved path leaves Trail Ridge Road and climbs over gentle terrain high above tree line.

Start: Rock Cut
Hiking time: 30 minutes to 1 hour
Distance: 0.8 mile out-and-back
Difficulty: Very easy
Other trail users: Wheelchairs, strollers
Maps: Trails Illustrated #200: Rocky Mountain National Park; USGS Trail Ridge
Highlights: Alpine plants, Mushroom Rocks, Toll Memorial peak finder
Elevations trailhead to Roger Toll Memorial: 12,110 feet to 12,310 feet (+200 feet)

Finding the trailhead: From the Fall River Entrance Station in Estes Park, drive 3.9 miles and turn right to stay on US 34 West. Continue 12.8 miles on US 34 / Trail Ridge Road to parking on the left. The trailhead is located on the other side of the road (GPS: 40 24.638, -105 43.840).

The Hike

Rock Cut is the highest trailhead in Rocky Mountain National Park and one of the busiest. Rock blasted from Rock Cut during road construction was used for road buttress across from the trailhead and also dumped nearby on the alpine tundra. The result is a natural-looking but unnaturally abundant accumulation of ideal rock habitat for cute, round-eared rabbit relatives called pika. Take care when crossing the road and watch the pika from above, along the retaining wall.

Thousands of people walking on embattled tundra plants would damage them significantly. Therefore, in this Tundra Protection Zone, stay on the paved trail.

The best diversity of tundra plants along the trail occurs at the trailhead, the most sheltered place for low-angle, tripod-using, wait-for-the-miserable-wind-to-quit photography of flowers. Typical of this area are some larger tundra species: purple fringe, sky pilot, bistort, and alpine sunflower.

For the first 0.25 mile, the edge of the asphalt is crowded by cushion plants pioneering the wind-scoured rock fields. Pink moss campion predominates, with white alpine sandwort also heroically struggling to bring life to the barren domain of the bitter wind. Watch for patterns of tundra flowers growing amid lines of jagged rocks (felsenmeer) heaved together and thrust up by the freezing and thawing of the ground.

The progress of this effort can be judged a short way up the trail, where an abandoned road dating from the construction of Trail Ridge Road comes in from the left. Quarry rock was transported along this road in the early 1930s. Although the twin ruts of truck tires are still obvious in the shape of the ground, the cushion plants have made equally obvious progress in covering the surface.

The path's beginning steepness distresses many motorists, who drive quickly and easily from oxygen-rich air at low altitude to thin air at high altitude and then attempt this hike. After the grade flattens, a spur path takes hikers to Mushroom Rocks, caprock formations unusual in this park. White feldspar that fractures easily into plates makes up most of the rock below caps of hard schist, more resistant to wind and temperature erosion.

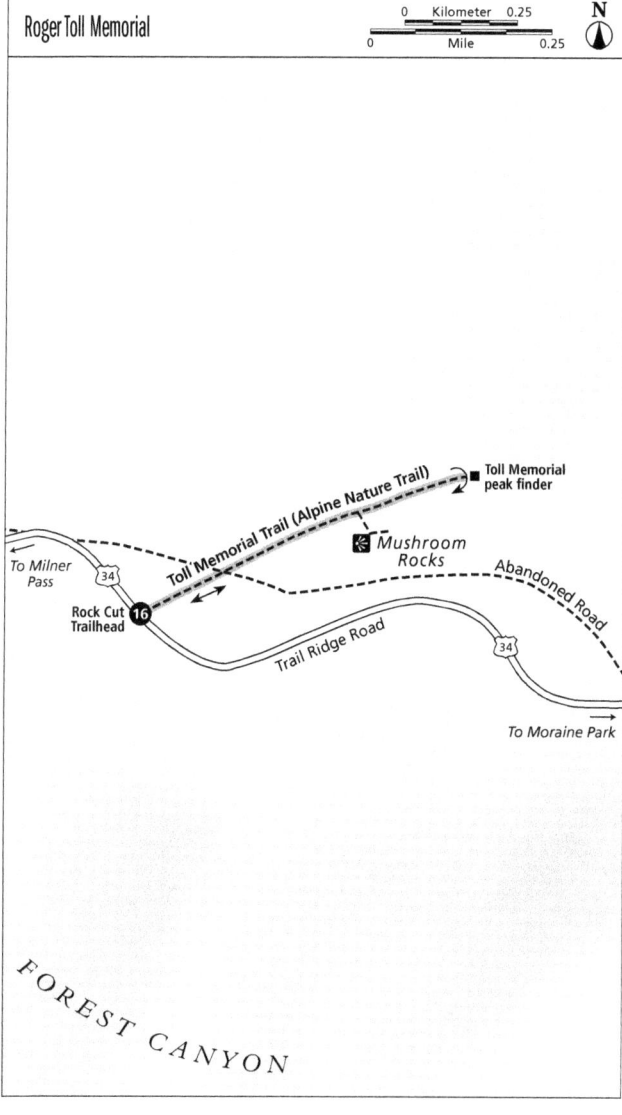

Stark color contrast and mushroom shapes make the rocks very photogenic. Less obvious is the pattern of cushion plants standing out against an unusual background of white rock chips along the trail west of Mushroom Rocks.

The last half of the trail is relatively flat until the last scramble up a rock outcrop to the peak finder that memorializes Roger Toll, the third park superintendent, who envisioned the building of Trail Ridge Road. The easier grade relieves the lungs, but does not help skin chilled by wind and low temperature and scorched by UV radiation. Appropriate clothing and sunscreen greatly enhance your enjoyment of the high-altitude tundra.

Miles and Directions

- **0.0** From the parking area, cross Trail Ridge Road and start your hike at Rock Cut Trailhead on north side of the road.
- **0.25** Spur path to right leads to Mushroom Rocks.
- **0.4** Reach Toll Memorial peak finder by scrambling to the top of rocks. Return the way you came.
- **0.8** Arrive back at Rock Cut Trailhead.

17 Deer Mountain

Deer Mountain divides Horseshoe Park and Beaver Meadows and offers views of the Mummy Range, Continental Divide, and Estes Park.

Start: Deer Mountain Trailhead
Hiking time: 4 to 5 hours
Distance: 6 miles out-and-back
Difficulty: Easy to moderate
Other trail users: Human foot traffic only
Maps: Trails Illustrated #200: Rocky Mountain National Park; USGS Estes Park

Highlights: Trailside and summit views of the Mummy Range, Continental Divide, and Estes Park
Elevations trailhead to Deer Mountain: 8,926 feet to 10,027 feet (+1,101 feet)

Finding the trailhead: From the Fall River Entrance Station in Estes Park, drive 3.9 miles and turn left onto US 36. The trailhead is just past this intersection, on the left. There is no parking lot, so park on the shoulder on either side of the road (GPS: 40 23.218, -105 36.594).

The Hike

This summit hike features enough elevation gain to provide a workout without wearing you out. The first mile crosses open terrain with a good trail and views south of the park's high peaks including Longs Peak, Pagoda Mountain, and McHenrys Peak. Looking north, left of the trail, the Mummy Range edges the sky.

The trail gains most of its elevation in the forested, rocky switchbacks between the first and second mile. A massive rock cairn tops the expansive summit. Pull up a

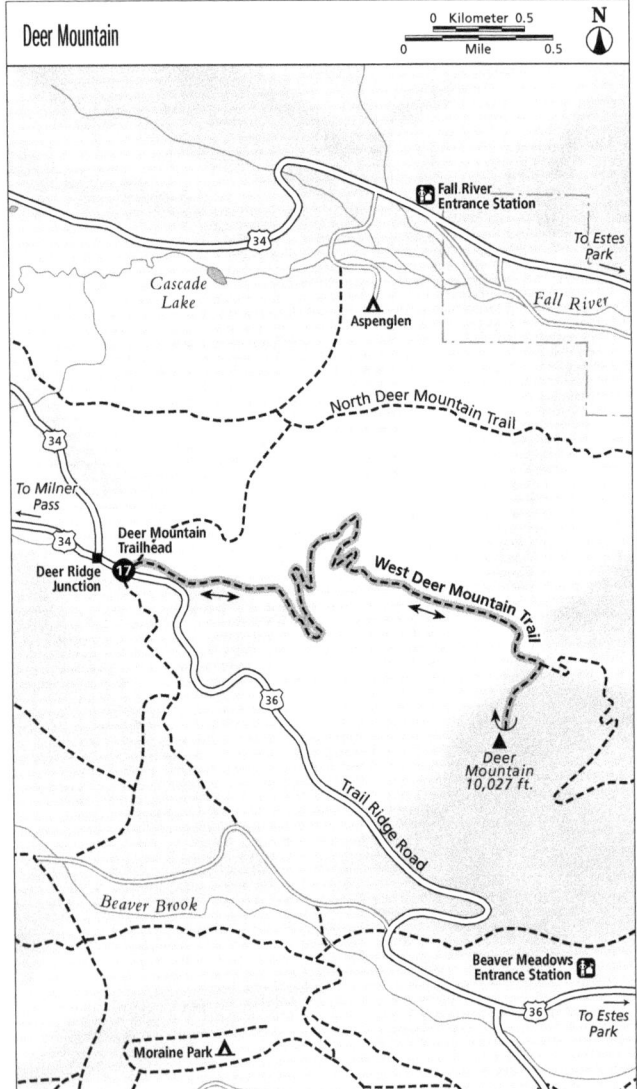

rock and enjoy more views of the Continental Divide to the west and Estes Park in the valley to the east.

Miles and Directions

- **0.0** From the Deer Mountain Trailhead, hike northeast on West Deer Mountain Trail.
- **0.1** The trail heads east with Deer Mountain in view straight ahead. At the trail junction with North Deer Mountain Trail, which leads to Aspenglen Campground, continue straight and east toward Deer Mountain.
- **0.8** Reach the first switchback. From here, the trail turns north and begins to rise steeply in alternating north and south switchbacks, east toward the summit ridge.
- **2.1** Continue as the trail eases gently east-southeast.
- **2.8** At a trail junction, turn right toward the summit. The East Deer Mountain Trail to Estes Park (not your route) goes left at the junction, so don't miss this important right turn.
- **3.0** Arrive at the rocky summit of Deer Mountain. Return the way you came.
- **6.0** Arrive back at the trailhead.

Kawuneeche Entrance and West Side of Trail Ridge Road (Grand Lake)

18 Big Meadows and Granite Falls

Tonahutu Creek slides over granite slabs at Granite Falls, then continues to Big Meadows and Grand Lake.

Start: Green Mountain Trailhead
Hiking time: 7 to 8 hours
Distance: 10.2 miles out-and-back
Difficulty: Easy to strenuous
Other trail users: Equestrians
Maps: Trails Illustrated #200: Rocky Mountain National Park; USGS Grand Lake
Highlights: Big Meadows, wildlife
Elevations trailhead to Granite Falls: 8,800 feet to 9,740 feet (+940 feet)

Finding the trailhead: From the Kawuneeche Entrance Station in Grand Lake, drive north on US 34 / Trail Ridge Road 2.5 miles to the parking lot and trailhead on right (GPS: 40 18.445, -105 50.471).

The Hike

Granite Falls slips down polished granite bedrock in several tiers and then cascades downstream between mossy banks in the remote Tonahutu Creek Valley (Tonahutu means "Big Meadow" in Arapaho) on the western side of Rocky Mountain National Park. A plunge pool at the bottom completes this pretty waterfall. This recommended hike passes through burned forests and Big Meadows, the park's largest montane ecosystem and home to mule deer and elk, before reaching the 50-foot-high slide waterfall. Look for moose along the waterways and on the trail. Do not approach them.

Although the hike gains nearly 1,000 feet of elevation, the rise is spread out, making a gradual ascent that never gets too steep. This area is ideal for a short backpack to nearby wilderness campsites, including Granite Falls, Lower Granite Falls, Sunrise, and Sunset.

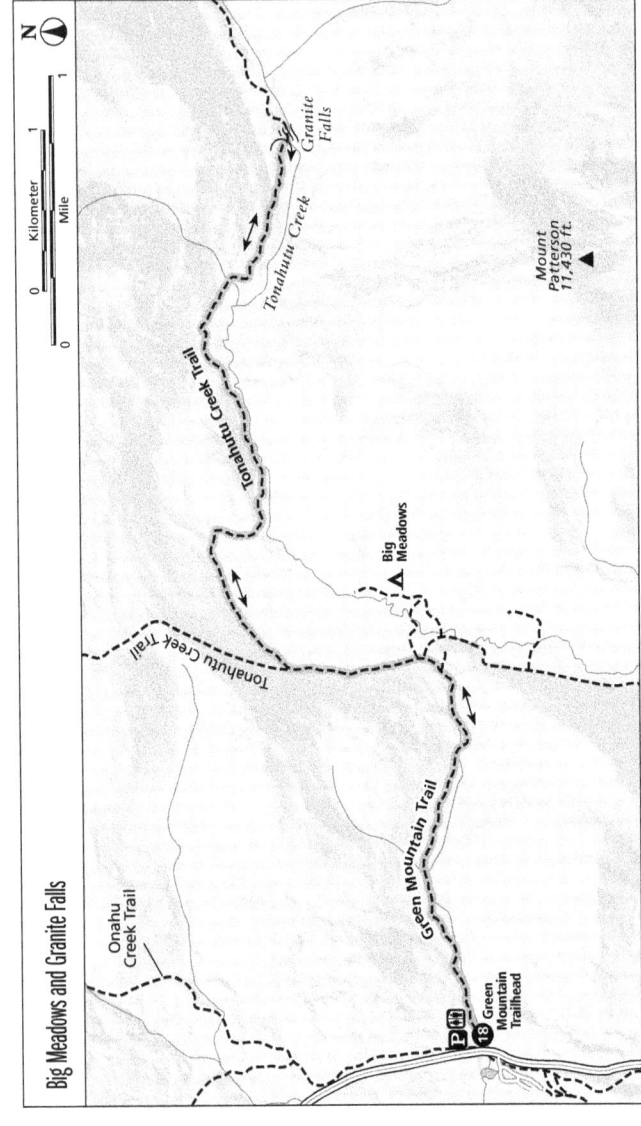

Miles and Directions

0.0 Begin at Green Mountain Trailhead and hike east through woods on Green Mountain Trail.

1.8 Reach junction with Tonahutu Creek Trail on west side of Big Meadows. Go left on it and hike north, keeping meadows to right. Watch for moose in meadows and on trail.

2.3 Reach junction with Onahu Creek Trail at north end of meadows. Keep right on Tonahutu Creek Trail toward Flattop Mountain and hike east.

3.0 Cross creek on footbridge.

4.4 Reach second creek crossing on footbridge.

5.1 Arrive at signed Granite Falls. Return the way you came.

10.2 Arrive back at trailhead.

19 Coyote Valley

Short and flat, this walkway, accessible by stroller and wheelchair, offers a delightful meander along the Colorado River through a variety of water-dependent habitats.

Start: Coyote Valley Trailhead
Hiking time: 30 minutes to 1 hour
Distance: 1.6 miles out-and-back
Difficulty: Very easy
Other trail users: Wheelchairs, strollers
Maps: Trails Illustrated #200: Rocky Mountain National Park; USGS Grand Lake
Highlights: Colorado River, views of Never Summer Range, wildlife
Elevations trailhead to turn-around point: 8,846 feet to 8,846 feet (+0 feet)

Finding the trailhead: From the Kawuneeche Entrance Station in Grand Lake, drive 5.4 miles north on US 34 / Trail Ridge Road to the parking lot and trailhead on left (GPS: 40 20.670, -105 51.500).

The Hike

Of the 297 bridges that carry hikers over streams in Rocky Mountain National Park, the bridge at the beginning of the Coyote Valley Trail may be the most elaborate, a humbler version of the magnificent Carriage Path bridges in Acadia National Park. This structure across the Colorado River leads to a wheelchair-accessible path along the level floodplain. Many benches and signs help visitors to appreciate and understand the riverside environment on the west side of Rocky Mountain National Park. Broad loops, detours, and cul-de-sacs provide variety in hiking to the trail's end and back.

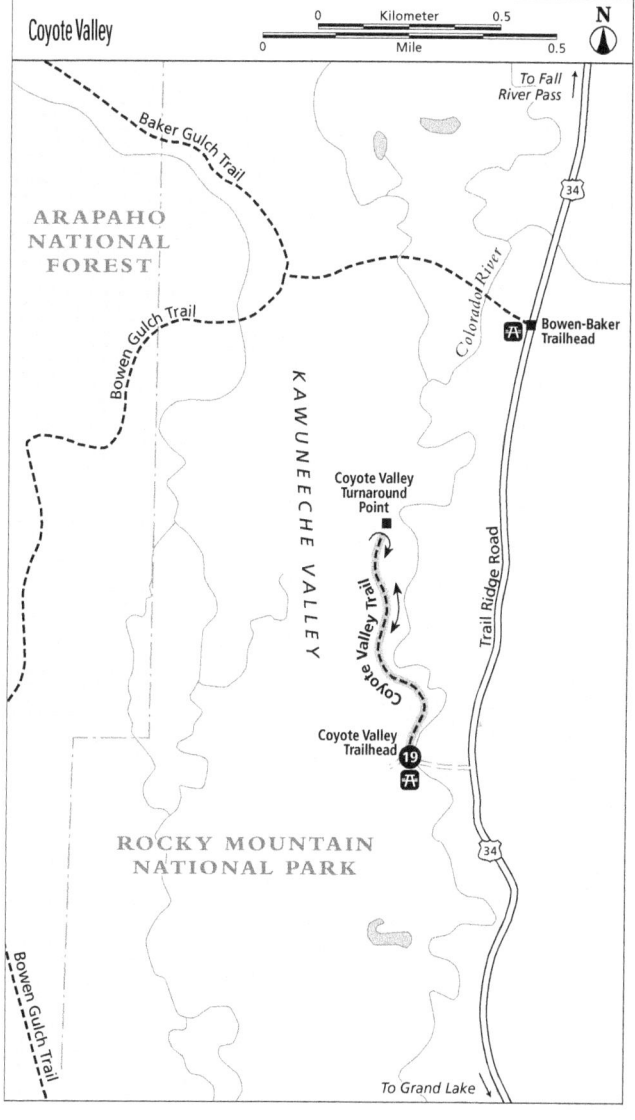

Miles and Directions

0.0 Start at Coyote Valley Trailhead.
0.8 Arrive at trail's end. Turn around to retrace the route.
1.6 Arrive back at Coyote Valley Trailhead.

20 Lulu City Site

A ramble along the peaceful headwaters of the Colorado River passes faint ruins of mining dreams set in pastoral majesty.

Start: Colorado River Trailhead
Hiking time: 4 to 5 hours
Distance: 7.4 miles out-and-back
Difficulty: Easy to moderate
Other trail users: Equestrians
Maps: Trails Illustrated #200: Rocky Mountain National Park; USGS Fall River Pass

Highlights: Shipler Mine, Lulu City
Elevations trailhead to Lulu City Site: 9,010 feet to 9,310 feet (+300 feet)

Finding the trailhead: From the Kawuneeche Entrance Station in Grand Lake, drive 9.4 miles north on US 34 / Trail Ridge Road to the parking lot and trailhead on left (GPS: 40 24.060, -105 50.920).

The Hike

Lulu City was never a city, and it was never a lulu. Lulu City was a vain hope that silver deposits in the Never Summer Range would be rich enough to exploit profitably. The streets laid out on paper in 1880 never passed more than the few buildings it took to serve 50 to 200 residents until the community's complete abandonment by 1884. These buildings are gone, and the few remaining logs and stone foundations and rusting bits of mining machinery are not obvious.

Distracted by the rich scenery, hikers often give no thought to the riches sought by Lulu City founders and residents. Even history enthusiasts usually are more impressed by the unbankable riches of wildflower color and jagged, snow-accented skyline than by the hopes of silver miners.

At 0.6 mile from the trailhead is the site of the old Phantom Valley guest ranch, where a trail to Red Mountain splits left from the trail to Lulu City and La Poudre Pass. The way to Lulu City continues fairly level along the Colorado River. Willows and other floodplain plants line the trail, and the workings of beavers are obvious. Human workings also appear in an 1880s mine site to the right of the trail beyond the split.

Shipler Mine, at 2.5 miles, preceded Lulu City and lasted until 1914. It likely was no more successful at producing silver, but Joe Shipler loved the land and hung on despite lack of riches, a common story even today in Grand County. He built his first sod-roofed cabin in 1876 and over the years managed to peck 100 yards into the granite of Shipler Mountain. Very lucky hikers may see mountain sheep amid the rubble of Shipler's mining efforts. (Stay out of all old mines; they are not safe.)

Passing on a level grade beyond the cabins, the trail follows a stage road that ran to Lulu City before heading northwest over Thunder Pass to Walden, Colorado. When at last the trail climbs above the valley floor, the shade of subalpine forest through which you walk is welcome. The trail forks at a junction 3.5 miles from the trailhead. The right-hand fork goes to the eroded volcanic rock of Little Yellowstone Canyon and La Poudre Pass. The left-hand fork heads back downhill through switchbacks for about 0.2 mile to the meadow that contained Lulu City. The Thunder Pass Trail continues through the meadow and past a steep connecting trail up to the La Poudre Pass Trail.

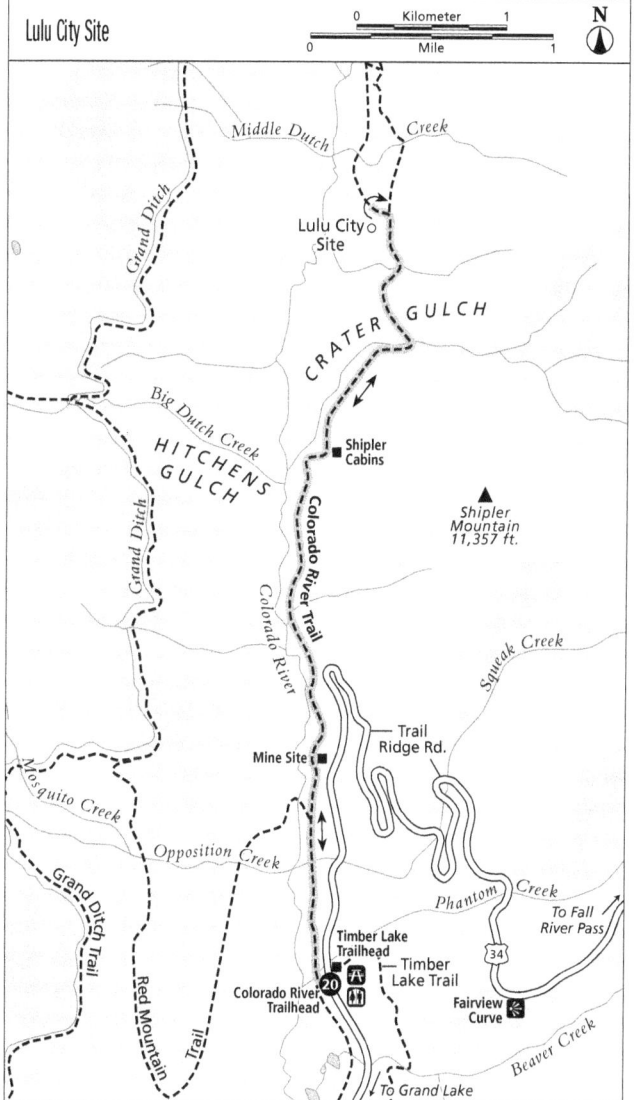

Miles and Directions

- **0.0** Start at Colorado River Trailhead. Hike north on Colorado River Trail.
- **2.5** Shipler Mine is not particularly obvious, which is just as well; mine workings are dangerous.
- **3.5** The trail splits; take left fork downhill.
- **3.7** Arrive at Lulu City site. Turn around to retrace your steps.
- **7.4** Arrive back at Colorado River Trailhead.

21 Mount Ida

A trek across alpine tundra climbs above Milner Pass with expansive views of the Never Summer Range.

Start: Poudre Lake Trailhead
Hiking time: 6 to 7 hours
Distance: 9.4 miles out-and-back
Difficulty: Easy to very strenuous
Other trail users: Human foot traffic only
Maps: Trails Illustrated #200: Rocky Mountain National Park; USGS Grand Lake
Highlights: Alpine tundra, good views of Never Summer Range
Elevations trailhead to Mount Ida: 10,759 feet to 12,882 feet (+2,123 feet)

Finding the trailhead: From the Kawuneeche Entrance Station in Grand Lake, drive north on US 34 / Trail Ridge Road for 16 miles to Milner Pass, parking, and the trailhead on right (GPS: 40 25.218, -105 48.685).

The Hike

Trail Ridge Road is the highest continuous paved road in the country, crossing the Continental Divide at 10,759-foot Milner Pass. Overlooks along Trail Ridge Road afford excellent views of Mount Ida and other peaks above the Gorge Lakes cirque on the east side of the peak. Milner Pass was named for T. J. Milner, who surveyed the area while in search of a route between Salt Lake City and Denver. Mount Ida, "The Mountain of the Goddess," was likely named for Mount Ida of Greek mythology. Views from the peak are never ending, with the Never Summer Mountains to the west, the Mummy Range to the north, and the Front Range to the south. Bighorn sheep are common on the upper slopes, and marmots scamper through the rocks at the summit.

Most of this hike is above timberline and open to the elements, contouring the mountainside along the Continental Divide. Do not attempt this hike in inclement weather or anytime lightning danger exists, as there is no quick escape route. The trail fades toward the summit, so if you lose your way, head east/uphill to the Divide and follow it until you pick up the trail.

Miles and Directions

- **0.0** Begin at the trailhead and hike east and south up switchbacks.
- **0.6** Pass the Ute Trail, a signed cutoff to Fall River Pass on the left, and continue south-southeast toward Mount Ida. Contour the mountainside under unranked Points 11881 and 12150.
- **2.7** Bear right at a cairn to stay on the correct trail. The upper trail is a social trail that peters out. Take the lower trail, which descends to a saddle.
- **3.3** Reach the saddle (12,000 feet) and hike upslope south-southeast on the trail.
- **3.6** Gain the ridge and continue along the rim of the cirque, as the trail fades to a cairned mix of dirt, talus, and tundra. Left of the trail, Trail Ridge Road is visible in the distance, with Sundance Mountain beyond.
- **3.9** Hike upslope southeast and follow the rim of the next cirque, overlooking Gorge Lakes. The rocky summit of Mount Ida is just ahead.
- **4.7** Arrive at ranked Mount Ida. Return the way you came.
- **9.4** Arrive back at the trailhead.

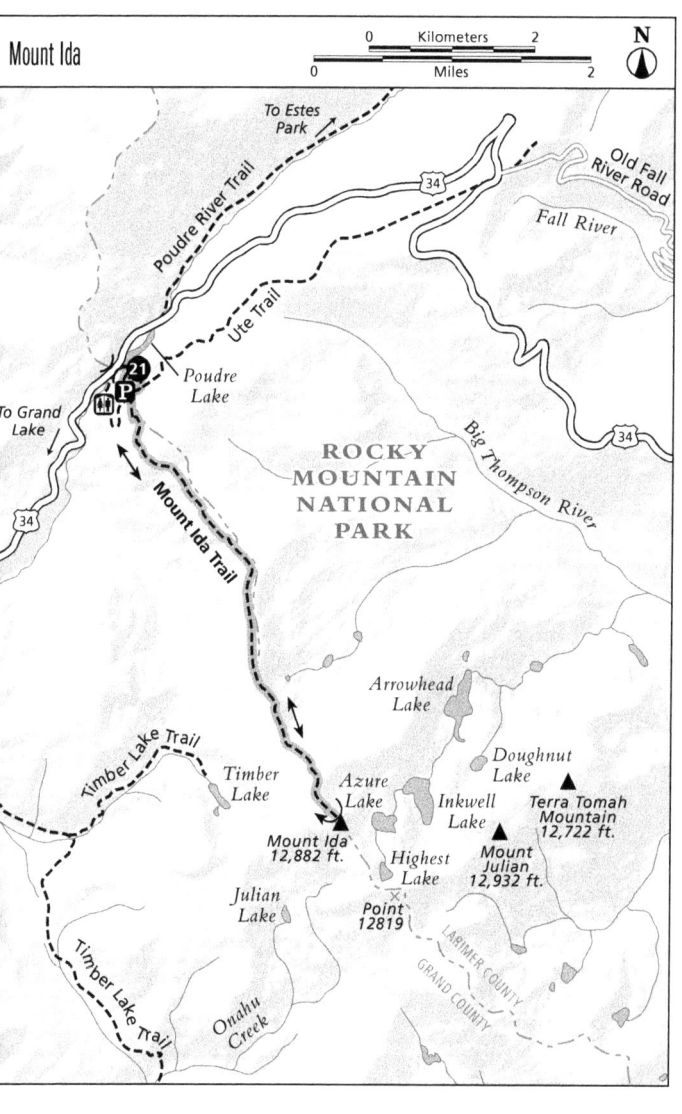

Wild Basin Entrance (Allenspark)

22 Sandbeach Lake

Enjoy spectacular mountain scenery and Colorado's highest sandy beach alongside a lofty lake on the northern edge of Wild Basin.

Start: Sandbeach Lake Trailhead
Hiking time: 6 to 7 hours
Distance: 8.6 miles out-and-back
Difficulty: Easy to very strenuous
Other trail users: Equestrians
Maps: Trails Illustrated #200: Rocky Mountain National Park; USGS Allens Park

Highlights: Sandy beach, mountain views
Elevations trailhead to Sandbeach Lake: 8,315 feet to 10,283 feet (+1,968 feet)

Finding the trailhead: From the Wild Basin Entrance Station in Allenspark, locate the parking lot and trailhead on CO 115 opposite the entrance station (GPS: 40 13.1879, -105 32.0624).

The Hike

Sandbeach Lake, lying on a wide bench below Mount Orton, is exactly that—a glacial lake bordered by a soft, sandy beach on its north and east shorelines. Visit the unique, 16.5-acre lake on a summer weekend and the scene isn't much different than the swim beach at Lake Pueblo or Chatfield Reservoir with hikers tanning on beach towels and kids frolicking in the frigid water. The 50-foot-deep lake, one of the deepest in the national park, was expanded by an earthen dam before the area became a national park in 1915, with the water stored for farmland irrigation. After the Lawn Lake Dam failed in 1982, the park removed the dam, leaving little trace of its existence. The sandy beach was deposited during its dammed years.

The hike to Sandbeach Lake follows a well-marked trail with mostly easy grades. The lake area usually isn't snow free until mid-June. With eight wilderness campsites and a group site, the trail and lake are also popular with backpackers. Besides the alpine beach, the lake offers astounding views of the surrounding mountains, including Longs Peak and neighboring Mount Meeker to the north.

Miles and Directions

- **0.0** Start at the Sandbeach Trailhead on the north side of the parking lot opposite the Wild Basin entrance station. Hike north on Sandbeach Trail and after 150 feet, keep right at a trail junction and hike up the steep trail to the top of the Copeland Moraine, a rocky moraine left by a large glacier that filled Wild Basin. Continue west atop the moraine through a pine and aspen forest.
- **1.3** Reach a junction with a trail on the right that leads northeast to Meeker Park. Continue straight, passing two backcountry campsites—Hole-in-the-Wall and Campers Creek.
- **2.4** Cross Campers Creek, jog left, and continue west on the trail past two more backcountry campsites—Beaver Mill and Hunters Creek.
- **3.4** Reach a crossing over Hunters Creek, which begins at Keplinger Lake below the south slope of Longs Peak. Continue northwest on the trail.
- **4.3** Reach the north shore of Sandbeach Lake, passing a hitching rack and four sites at Sandbeach Lake Wilderness Campsite. After working on your alpine tan, return the way you came.
- **8.6** Arrive back at the trailhead.

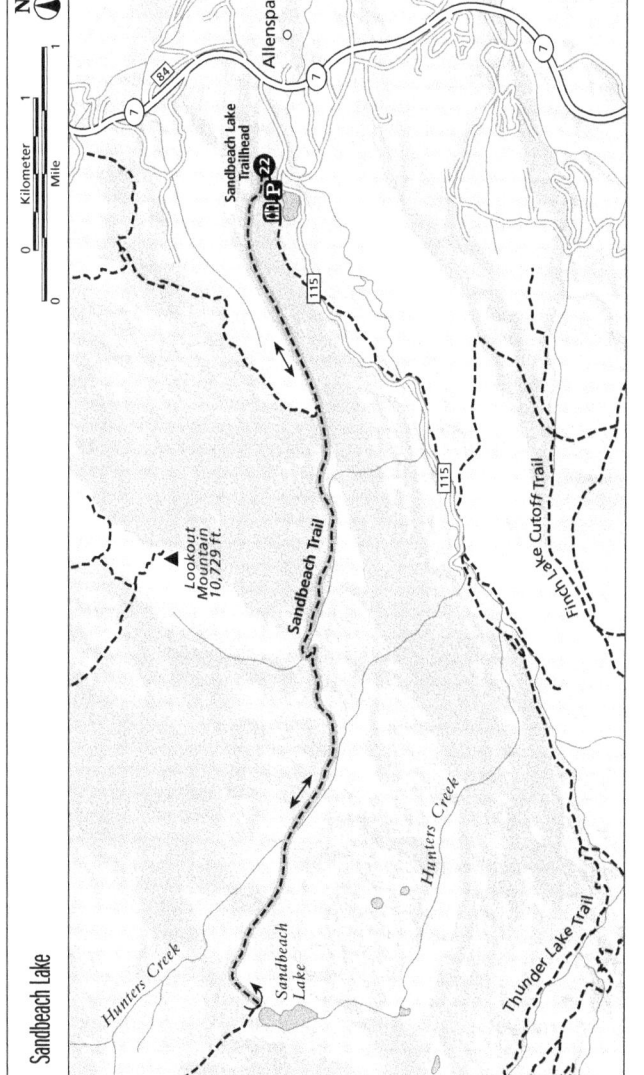

23 Ouzel Falls

Rarely removed from falling water music, this wilderness walk passes through enclosing woods to plummeting falls.

Start: Wild Basin Trailhead
Hiking time: 3 to 4 hours
Distance: 5.5 miles out-and-back
Difficulty: Easy to moderate
Other trail users: Equestrians
Maps: Trails Illustrated #200: Rocky Mountain National Park; USGS Allens Park
Highlights: Abundant wildflowers, noisy white-water stream, waterfalls
Elevations trailhead to Ouzel Falls: 8,500 feet to 9,460 feet (+960 feet)

Finding the trailhead: From the Wild Basin Entrance Station in Allenspark, drive 2.1 miles on CO 115 to a ranger station and parking at road's end. The trailhead is at the south end of the lower parking lot (GPS: 40 12.4667, -105 33.99).

The Hike

Although dawn or earlier is usually the best time to start hiking in Rocky Mountain National Park, this painful practice is unnecessary for a hike to Ouzel Falls, which does not exhibit significant mountain views.

The low, bright light of early morning that illuminates mountain vistas so dramatically is not the best light for viewing shady streamside vistas along the trail to Wild Basin's most popular hiking destination. Sunny skies pour too much light on raging white streams, making so much contrast between water and woods that it is very difficult for your eyes to perceive the whole scene at once. Toward midday the sun will be higher in the sky and often dimmed by clouds, casting an even light by which it is easier to appreciate the wonders of Wild Basin forests.

The lower light level under cloudy skies also permits photographers to steady their cameras on tripods, rocks, or bridge railings to use a slow shutter speed. This slow speed allows moving water to flow into fuzziness while surrounding solid objects remain still during the opening of the camera shutter.

The Wild Basin trails are rich in wildflower species. Watch in particular (in early July) for small pink Calypso or fairy slipper orchids at trailside near Calypso Cascades. A shaft of sun may penetrate the shade to spotlight one of these orchids.

The burned area beyond Calypso Cascades exhibits the lush green of shrubs and flowers that grew up after forest shade was removed. You are likely to see deer here, as well as marmots and ground squirrels. Appropriately, fireweed is very abundant, but deer often eat its bright magenta blossoms, disappointing hikers who expect to enjoy masses of color. The colors of flowers, leaves, and burned wood blend more pleasingly under overcast rather than sunny skies.

At the bridge over Ouzel Creek below Ouzel Falls (reconstructed after a 2013 flood), leave the main trail to climb along the left bank to the base of the falls. Here you may find the falls graced by the presence of colorful wildflowers.

Ouzel Falls is named for a dull gray bird that is a bit smaller than a robin and shaped like a wren. Ouzels also are called dippers because they fly from under the water to land on a rock and perform an entertaining bobbing dance. They stay in the water or just above it rather than flying over the land. You are likely to see ouzels along any of Wild Basin's streams.

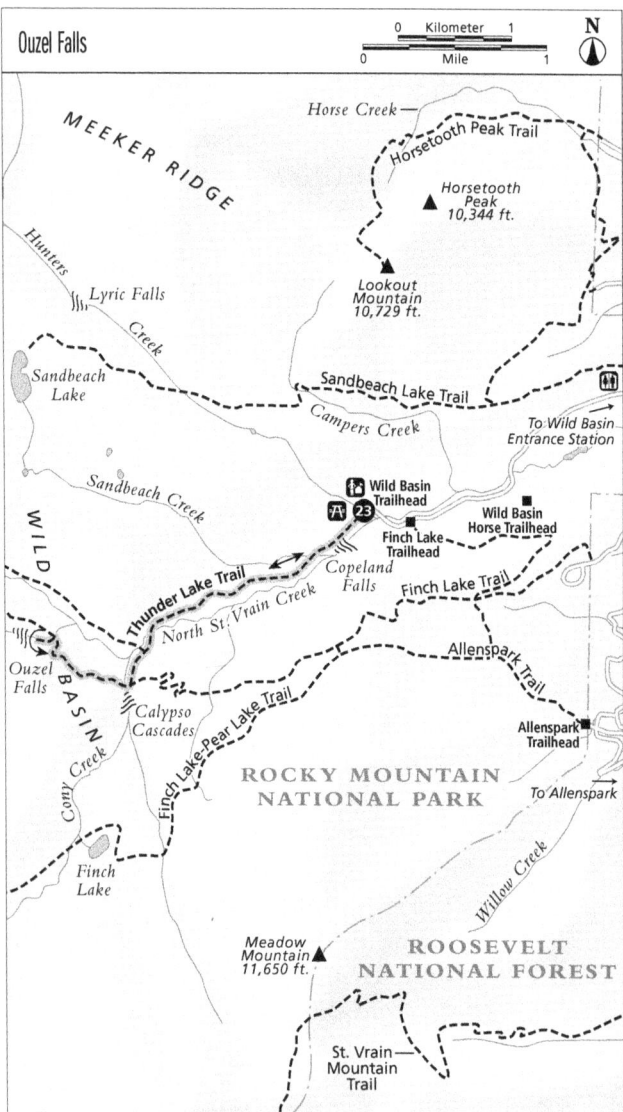

Miles and Directions

0.0 Begin at Wild Basin Trailhead, located across parking lot from ranger station. Hike west on Thunder Lake Trail along North St. Vrain Creek.

0.3 Go left off main trail on a signed spur toward Lower Copeland Falls.

0.4 Arrive at Lower Copeland Falls. Return to trail and go left toward Upper Copeland Falls (signed).

0.5 Arrive at Upper Copeland Falls. Continue on side trail to rejoin signed main trail.

0.6 Rejoin Thunder Lake Trail and go left (signed) up wide trail right of creek.

1.5 Trail bends left and crosses creek on footbridge to "Lovers Leaps." Continue uphill on trail alongside Cony Creek.

1.8 Reach junction with signed Allenspark–Wild Basin Trail on left. Go right on three bridges over Calypso Cascades. Continue west across wooded slopes on Thunder Lake Trail.

2.8 Arrive at footbridge with Ouzel Falls to left. Scramble up a short side trail on the left side of Ouzel Creek to the base of Ouzel Falls. After viewing, return the way you came, omitting the side trip to Copeland Falls.

5.5 Arrive back at trailhead.

24 Bluebird Lake

The Bluebird Lake Trail passes Calypso Cascades, Ouzel Falls, and Ouzel Lake before climbing to a sparkling alpine lake in a cirque below the Continental Divide.

Start: Wild Basin Trailhead
Hiking time: 8 to 9 hours
Distance: 12.6 miles out-and-back
Difficulty: Easy to very strenuous
Other trail users: Equestrians to hitchrack only

Maps: Trails Illustrated #200: Rocky Mountain National Park; USGS Allens Park, Isolation Peak
Highlights: Waterfalls, mountain views
Elevations trailhead to Bluebird Lake: 8,500 feet to 10,978 feet (+2,478 feet)

Finding the trailhead: From the Wild Basin Entrance Station in Allenspark, drive 2.1 miles on CO 115 to a ranger station and parking at road's end. The trailhead is at the south end of the lower parking lot (GPS: 40 12.4667, -105 33.99).

The Hike

The Bluebird Lake Trail climbs to shimmering Bluebird Lake nestled in a glacier-carved cirque on the southern end of Wild Basin. Gaining nearly 2,500 feet of elevation, the hike follows rushing creeks, passes three waterfalls and Ouzel Lake, and crosses high meadows. Best done from mid-June through September, this hike also offers mountain views, wildlife, and solitude. Despite the park's popularity, the trail is never crowded, with most hikers only trekking to the waterfalls. Arrive early at the trailhead to grab a parking spot since the lot fills fast, especially on weekends.

The first hike section starts at Wild Basin Trailhead. Head west on Thunder Lake Trail past Lower and Upper

Copeland Falls, two small waterfalls on North St. Vrain Creek, to a footbridge over the creek. Climb south alongside Cony Creek, passing a horsetail cascade called "Lover's Leaps," to a junction with the Allenspark–Wild Basin Trail and the base of 200-foot-high Calypso Cascades. This waterfall, named for pink, fairy-slipper orchids, tumbles over boulders and fallen tree trunks. Continue another mile to roaring Ouzel Falls, one of Rocky Mountain National Park's most beautiful waterfalls. The 50-foot falls, a popular hiking destination, is named for the water ouzel or American dipper, a small bird that lives along frigid mountain streams. From the falls, follow Thunder Lake Trail another 0.5 mile to the Bluebird Lake Trail, which climbs through the burn scar of a 1978 wildfire. Higher is a side trail that visits shallow Chickadee Pond and Ouzel Lake, a lovely pond below the north face of 13,183-foot Mount Copeland. The last hike section climbs 1,000 feet from Ouzel Lake to Bluebird Lake, crossing open slopes sprinkled with wildflowers, traversing moist evergreen forests, and scrambling up polished slabs to an overlook above Bluebird Lake. The gorgeous lake reflects rugged peaks including Mahana Peak and Ouzel Peak on the Continental Divide. The now-pristine lake was enlarged by a dam for Longmont drinking water in the early 1920s. In 1974 it was ruled unsafe, and the National Park Service removed 5 million pounds of concrete by helicopter and restored the lake.

Miles and Directions

- **0.0** Start at the Wild Basin Trailhead. Follow Thunder Lake Trail west alongside the north bank of North St. Vrain Creek.
- **0.3** Reach Copeland Falls on the right. A short side path leads to the falls.

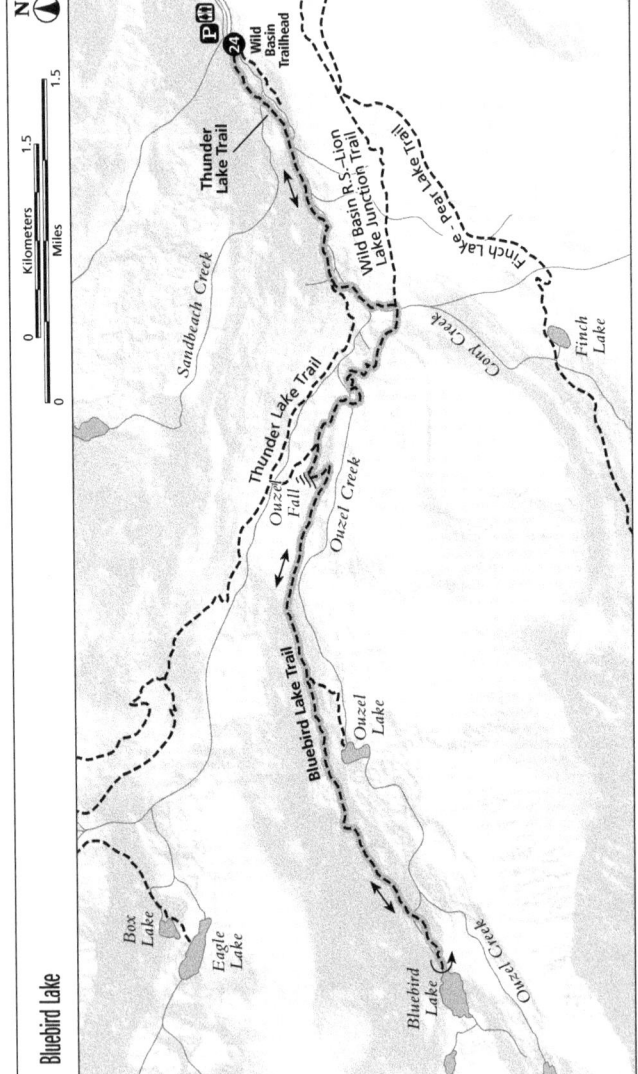

- **1.2** Reach a junction with a trail on the right. Go left, cross a bridge over the creek, and hike uphill alongside Cony Creek.
- **1.8** Arrive at a junction with the Allenspark–Wild Basin Trail. Go right to Calypso Cascades, a long, tumbling waterfall, on a boardwalk.
- **2.7** Continue west on Thunder Lake Trail for 0.9 mile to Ouzel Falls, one of the park's prettiest waterfalls, on the left. A rough trail heads left from a footbridge to a viewpoint below the falls. Continue west on the trail, contouring across the mountainside.
- **3.1** Reach the junction with Bluebird Lake Trail on the left. Go left on Bluebird Lake Trail and climb south up slopes to a rounded ridge. Continue southwest along the ridgetop.
- **4.5** Reach a trail junction on the left. The path heads 0.4 mile into the broad valley to tree-lined Ouzel Lake. Return to the junction and go left on Bluebird Lake Trail across a slope above Ouzel Lake and Chickadee Pond. The trail ascends through old forest below cliffs, then climbs up glacier-scraped rock ribs and gullies.
- **6.3** Reach a granite bench above the northeast side of Bluebird Lake. Revel in views west of mountains lining the rim of the cirque, including Mount Copeland, Ouzel Peak, and Mahana Peak. After lunch, return back down the trails the way you came.
- **12.6** Arrive back at the trailhead.

Other Entrances and Trailheads

25 West Creek Falls

Trudging steeply uphill at its beginning, this route drops almost as steeply before it moderates to a pleasant grade to secluded falls.

Start: Cow Creek Trailhead
Hiking time: 3 to 4 hours
Distance: 4.6 miles out-and-back
Difficulty: Easy to moderate
Other trail users: Equestrians
Maps: Trails Illustrated #200: Rocky Mountain National Park; USGS Glen Haven and Estes Park
Highlights: McGraw Ranch, West Creek Falls
Elevations trailhead to West Creek Falls: 7,820 feet to 8,100 feet (+280 feet)

Finding the trailhead: From downtown Estes Park, take MacGregor Avenue for 1 mile, where the road veers slightly right and becomes Devils Gulch Road. Continue 2.7 miles and bear left on McGraw Ranch Road. Drive 2.2 miles to the trailhead, on left. Parking is only permitted in the parking area at the trailhead. Do not park along the road beyond the ranch boundary (GPS: 40 25.876, -105 30.061).

The Hike

McGraw Ranch, one of the oldest in this area, was established in 1874. Cow Creek gained its name soon after, presumably from the stock on the ranch. Various architectural details of the ranch structures make good photo subjects and backgrounds for portraits.

Even a century ago it was obvious that catering to tourists made more economic sense than catering to cows. McGraw Ranch enabled many guests to experience the beauty of its out-of-the-way valley. The back of a horse was the favored vantage point of these guests.

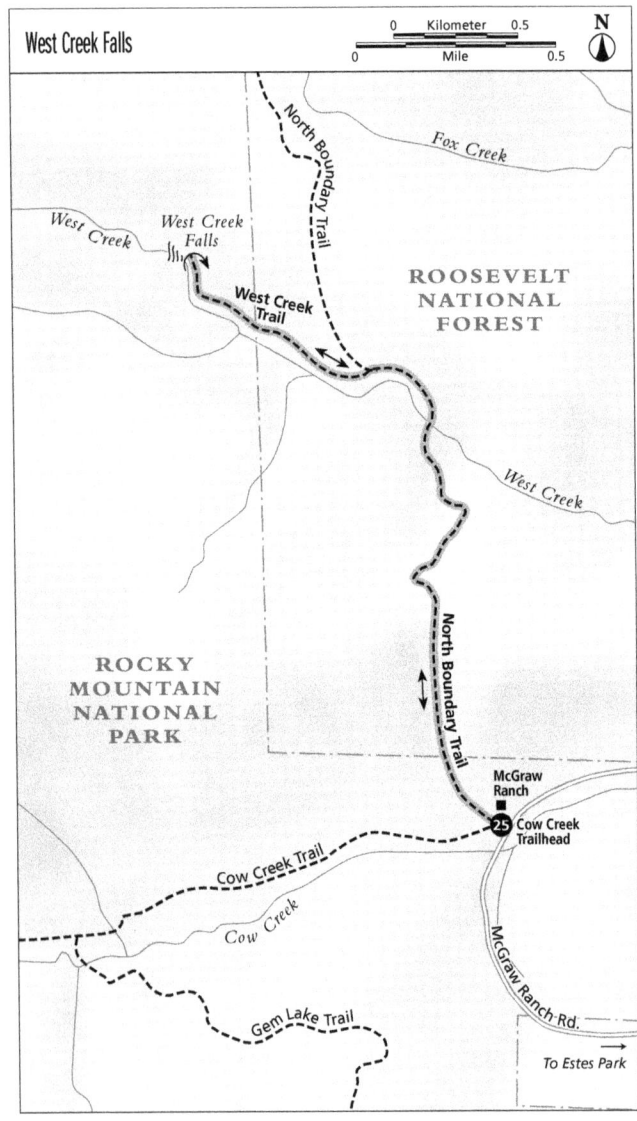

Just west of the ranch buildings, the North Boundary Trail to West Creek Falls heads right up a ridge, the route of guests content to let horses do the puffing and panting. From the low point on the ridge between West and Cow Creeks, the trail weaves back and forth steeply down through a Douglas-fir forest to West Creek. Across the creek, head left (west) at a trail intersection and walk a gentle grade along the bank to West Creek Falls. In this peaceful setting of a rocky amphitheater, the creek descends in two tiers.

Miles and Directions

0.0 Begin at Cow Creek Trailhead. Hike west through McGraw Ranch on Cow Creek Trail.
0.1 On west side of buildings, reach junction and turn right (north) on signed North Boundary Trail.
0.3 Enter Comanche Peak Wilderness, hike over ridge, descend into West Creek drainage, and cross footbridge over creek.
1.4 Reach junction and turn left on signed North Boundary Trail.
1.6 Reach junction and turn left toward West Creek Falls on signed side trail.
2.0 Enter Rocky Mountain National Park.
2.3 Arrive at West Creek Falls. Return the way you came.
4.6 Arrive back at the trailhead.

26 Bridal Veil Falls

Meadows and aspen groves surround the path to a waterfall easy to imagine from its name.

Start: Cow Creek Trailhead
Hiking time: 4 to 5 hours
Distance: 6.2 miles out-and-back
Difficulty: Easy to moderate
Other trail users: Equestrians as far as a hitching post below the falls
Maps: Trails Illustrated #200: Rocky Mountain National Park; USGS Estes Park
Highlights: Aspen-lined Cow Creek, Bridal Veil Falls
Elevations trailhead to Bridal Veil Falls: 7,820 feet to 8,800 feet (+980 feet)

Finding the trailhead: From downtown Estes Park, take MacGregor Avenue for 1 mile, where the road veers slightly right and becomes Devils Gulch Road. Continue 2.7 miles and bear left on McGraw Ranch Road. Drive 2.2 miles to the trailhead, on left. Parking is permitted only in the parking area at the trailhead. Do not park along the road beyond the ranch boundary (GPS: 40 25.876, -105 30.061).

The Hike

Cow Creek presumably was named for the livestock at McGraw Ranch, established in 1874. The cattle were gone long before McGraw Ranch became part of Rocky Mountain National Park in 1988. There were many cows along Cow Creek nonetheless—cow and bull elk.

You have an excellent chance of spotting elk along Cow Creek on the way to Bridal Veil Falls, particularly in winter, so if you have a telephoto lens and tripod, haul them along. The extra effort could yield a prizewinning photo.

The trail to the falls is relatively easy. The path meanders west from the trailhead, usually staying in the open meadows that are vital sources of food for elk. Usually free of winter snow, the path can be rather warm in the summer. Using sunscreen is a good idea throughout the year.

Hikers need not be particularly observant to see that the elk do not feed only on the grass. They also eat willows and streamside shrubs. The black scars on aspen bark are particularly obvious signs of elk dining. The double vertical scars show where elk use their lower incisors to strip bark from the trees. Light-colored wood indicates more recent feeding; it eventually turns black. The rough black scars contrasting with the smooth, nearly white aspen bark can create some interesting patterns for close-up photography.

Beavers also feed on the aspen and use it extensively to construct dams and lodges. Many beaver ponds slow the flow of Cow Creek, providing excellent opportunities in fall for reflection photos of aspen gold.

Actually spotting the beavers themselves will be a matter of luck. They are in significant danger from predators when they are out of the water, and they tend to do most of their cutting at night. The beavers are most active in summer and fall, when they store aspen and willow branches and trunks under the surface of the water. After winter freezes the surface, they reach their stores by an underwater entrance from their den or lodge.

Bridal Veil Falls is one of the prettiest in the park. It is especially spectacular in spring, when the torrent of melting snow rushes over the falls with so much force that the water gushes back into the air from the pool below the falls. In winter, the more subtle beauties of frozen splashes and streamside ice patterns create a lovely setting.

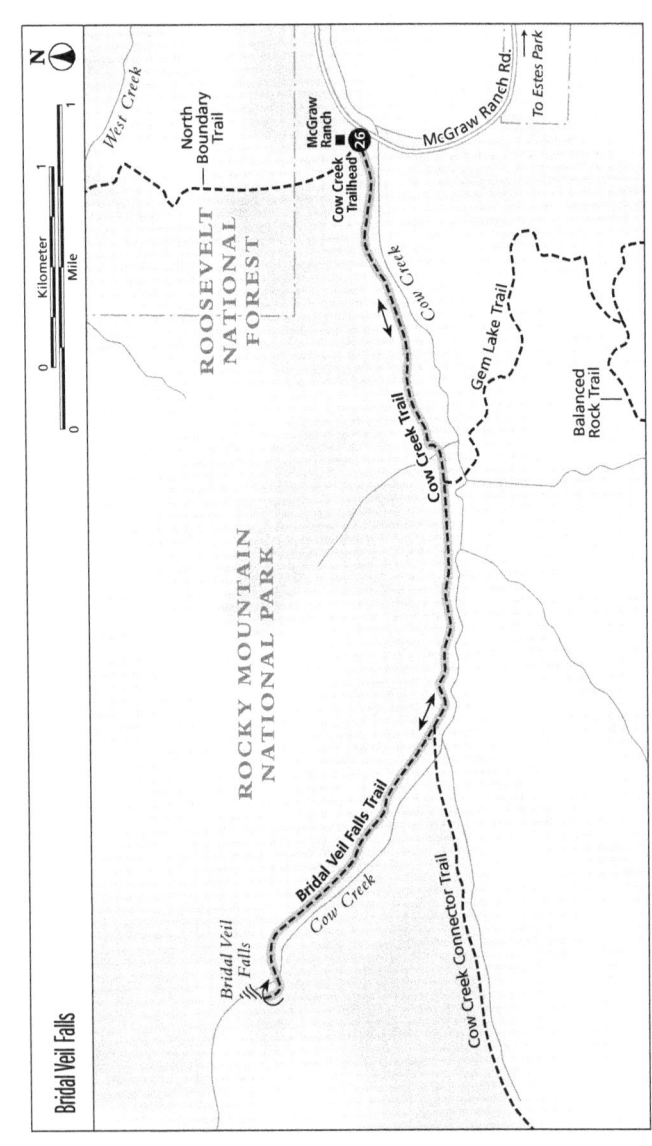

Miles and Directions

0.0 Begin at Cow Creek Trailhead. Hike past buildings at old McGraw Ranch and toilet.

0.1 Reach junction with North Boundary Trail at ranch. Go straight on Cow Creek Trail. Right turn goes to West Creek Falls. Continue west on old road that becomes singletrack trail.

1.2 Junction with Gem Lake Trail. Continue straight. Left heads to Gem Lake and Lumpy Ridge Trailhead.

1.9 Reach trail junction in bottom of valley. Go right on Bridal Veil Falls Trail. Left turn is Cow Creek Connector Trail, which leads to Black Canyon Trail.

2.9 Pass horse hitch and start up steep, rocky trail. Pay attention to stay on trail.

3.1 Reach base of Bridal Veil Falls. Return the way you came.

6.2 Arrive back at trailhead.

27 Gem Lake

This trail winds amid uncounted granite monoliths to a gem's setting on the east end of Lumpy Ridge.

Start: Lumpy Ridge Trailhead
Hiking time: 2 to 3 hours
Distance: 3.2 miles out-and-back
Difficulty: Easy to moderate
Other trail users: Equestrians
Maps: Trails Illustrated #200: Rocky Mountain National Park; USGS Glen Haven and Estes Park
Highlights: Unique rock formations, views of Longs Peak above Estes Valley, Gem Lake
Elevations trailhead to Gem Lake: 7,840 feet to 8,835 feet (+995 feet)

Finding the trailhead: From downtown Estes Park, drive north on MacGregor Avenue (which becomes Devils Gulch Road) for 1.9 miles and turn left on Lumpy Ridge Road. Continue 0.3 mile to parking and the trailhead (GPS: 40 23.803, -105 30.738).

The Hike

Popular throughout the year, Gem Lake is a particularly good hike for folks eager to experience spring on the trail. In Rocky Mountain National Park, the Gem Lake Trail sees spring first. Here is the place to observe pasqueflowers pushing their purple tulip heads through the forest duff. Watch for bitterbrush blooming first near the surface of rocks that are solar collectors, radiating heat to create early spring before the season arrives for most other plants.

Even the most unimaginative of hikers can see a pair of owls in the two huge granite pillars that rise above the trailhead on Lumpy Ridge. Equally obvious is Paul Bunyan's Boot about halfway to Gem Lake. Wind and mildly acidic rain have sculpted countless other abstract monoliths along the trail into formations fascinating to both romantic and prosaic minds. It is a natural playground for children, but parents need to supervise and warn kids to avoid falls from slick rocks.

Gem Lake is a small jewel in a big setting. Actually a large (0.2-acre) pothole in the granite, it has no inlet or outlet and averages a foot deep. Its beauty, therefore, is more subtle than that of the grand alpine lakes higher in the park. Notice the abstract color patterns of lichens at the base of the cliffs on the north shore. Limber pines frame the distant peaks.

Weathering of rocks atop the cliff above the lake has created remarkable patterns of potholes. The easiest way to reach these is to clamber very carefully up the less steep slope around the corner of the rock bulwark on the north side of the lake.

Climbing to the top of the cliff may also bring you closer to white-throated swifts, birds that look like cigars with swept-back wings. They dart at very high speeds over the water in pursuit of flying insects.

Miles and Directions

- **0.0** Start on the right side of the toilets at the Lumpy Ridge Trailhead. Following signs for "Gem Lake," go right on Lumpy Ridge Trail and hike north up a cliff-lined canyon.
- **0.5** Reach a junction with Black Canyon Trail. Go right on Gem Lake Trail and hike up the steep trail below cliffs with views south of Longs Peak and the Continental Divide peaks.
- **1.6** Reach the sandy west side of Gem Lake in a cliff-rimmed bowl. Return the way you came.
- **3.2** Arrive back at the trailhead.

28 MacGregor Falls

Black Canyon Creek flows southeast from Mummy Mountain, empties into the Big Thompson River, then cascades through a narrow passage, twists through boulders, and slip-slides over a granite slab in a frothy sheet at MacGregor Falls.

Start: Lumpy Ridge Trailhead
Hiking time: 4 to 5 hours
Distance: 6.2 miles out-and-back
Difficulty: Easy to moderate
Other trail users: Equestrians, to hitching post
Maps: Trails Illustrated #200: Rocky Mountain National Park; USGS Estes Park
Highlights: Views of Lumpy Ridge
Elevations trailhead to MacGregor Falls: 7,840 feet to 8,330 feet (+490 feet)

Finding the trailhead: From downtown Estes Park, drive north on MacGregor Avenue (which becomes Devils Gulch Road) for 1.9 miles and turn left on Lumpy Ridge Road. Continue 0.3 mile to parking and the trailhead (GPS: 40 23.803, -105 30.738).

The Hike

Black Canyon Creek dashes southeast down deep Black Canyon before rumbling over 20-foot McGregor Falls below craggy cliffs at Lumpy Ridge. The hike, following Black Canyon Trail and then the unmarked McGregor Falls Trail, is not hard to follow, but bring a map and pay attention as you hike to find the crucial, unsigned cutoff left at the junction with The Pear climber's path.

Miles and Directions

0.0 Begin at Lumpy Ridge Trailhead and hike west on Lumpy Ridge Trail over a ridge to Black Canyon Trail.

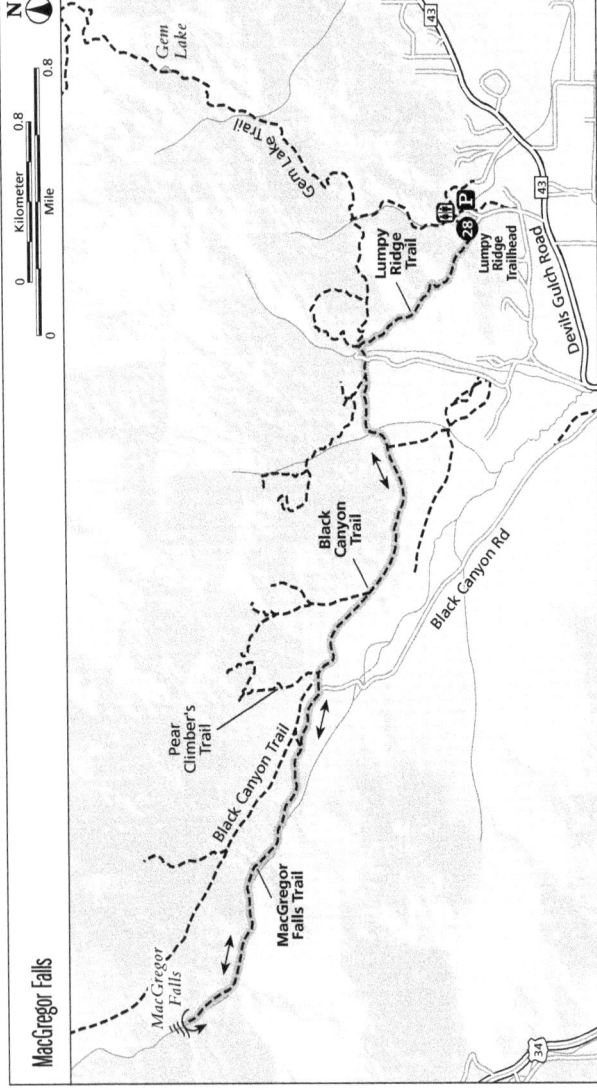

- **0.6** Reach junction with Black Canyon Trail. Go left on Black Canyon Trail and hike through grassland toward The Pear, passing obvious Lumpy Ridge rock formations like the Twin Owls.
- **0.7** Cross a closed road and rejoin trail on other side, then arrive at trail junction. Stay left on Black Canyon Trail.
- **1.5** Reach trail junction with climbing routes to right; continue straight.
- **1.8** Reach a pole where a social trail meanders straight ahead; bear right.
- **1.9** Reach junction on right with climber's trail to The Pear. The Pear is right and Black Canyon Trail continues straight. Look left for a cairn and follow faint trail southwest across meadow for 320 feet; join closed dirt road on other side. Walk west up ranch road.
- **2.3** Road ends at Black Canyon Creek. Continue west on trail to right (signed for MacGregor Falls). Follow trail along creek to left.
- **3.1** Arrive at base of MacGregor Falls in shady, rock-walled alcove. After viewing falls, return the way you came.
- **6.2** Arrive back at trailhead.

29 Lily Lake

A gentle, stroller-friendly trail follows the shoreline of scenic Lily Lake in a wide valley on the east side of Rocky Mountain National Park.

Start: Lily Lake Trailhead
Hiking time: 30 minutes to 1 hour
Distance: 0.8-mile loop
Difficulty: Very easy
Other trail users: Wheelchairs, strollers

Maps: Trails Illustrated #200: Rocky Mountain National Park; USGS Longs Peak
Highlights: Mountain views, Lily Lake
Elevations trailhead to Lily Lake: 8,930 feet to 8,930 feet (+0 feet)

Finding the trailhead: From the junction of US 36 and CO 7 in Estes Park, drive south for 6.3 miles on CO 7 and turn right to parking and the trailhead (GPS: 40 18.4003, -105 32.275).

The Hike

Lily Lake, lying on the eastern edge of Rocky Mountain National Park, is a lovely, 18-acre lake nestled in a valley against Lily Mountain's south flank. The lake, dammed and enlarged in 1915, was originally private property. The water and recreation rights were bought by Larimer County Parks & Open Lands and the Estes Valley Land Trust to protect the scenic lake from development.

The Lily Lake Trail explores the shoreline of the popular lake, offering stunning views of Longs Peak, Estes Cone, and Twin Sisters. The wide trail is easily traveled by wheelchairs and strollers. The restrooms, picnic tables, and pier here are also ADA accessible. The hike is kid-friendly

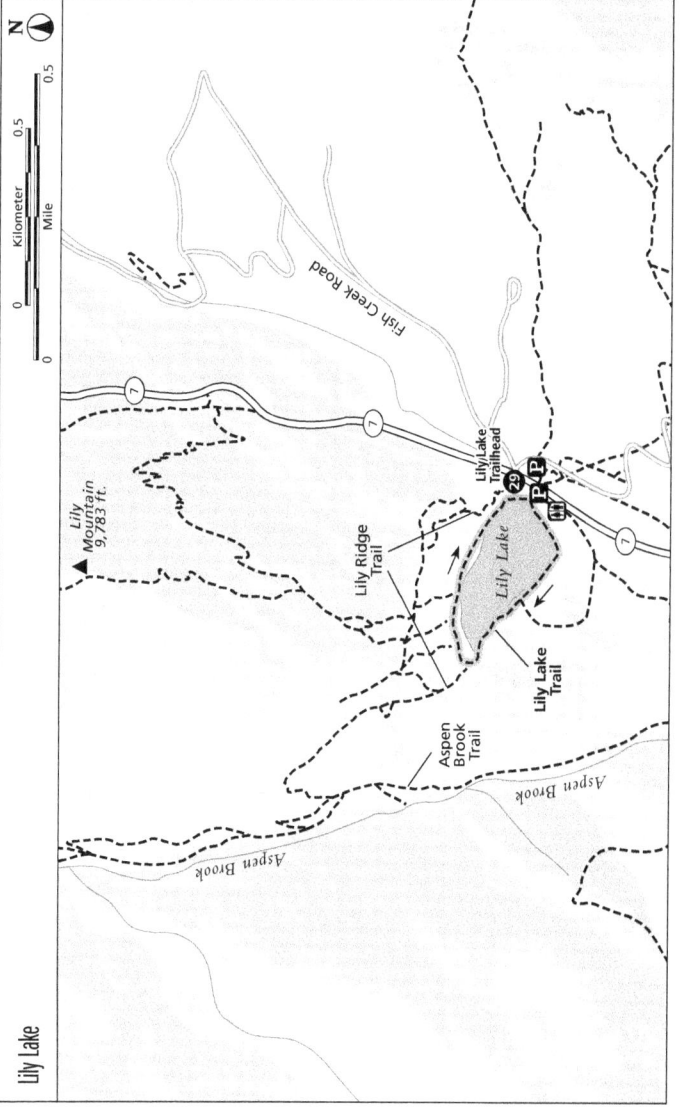

with minimal elevation gain and wildlife watching, including moose wading in the shallows. A couple of side trails, including Lily Ridge Trail, allow hikers to extend their adventure. Rock climbers also use the trail to reach a steep path to cliffs at Jurassic Park high on Lily Mountain.

Miles and Directions

- **0.0** Start at the Lily Lake Trailhead and go left (clockwise) on the trail. Hike along the lake's edge to a boardwalk over a marsh.
- **0.2** Reach a junction on the left with New Storm Pass Trail, which heads southwest to Estes Cone. Continue northwest along the lake's south shoreline.
- **0.4** Reach the junction with the Lily Ridge Trail on the left. Continue on the main trail, which bends right and follows the north shore of Lily Lake.
- **0.7** Reach a junction with the eastern end of Lily Ridge Trail. Keep right on the trail and cross a levee at the lake's eastern end.
- **0.8** Arrive back at the trailhead.

30 Peacock Pool and Columbine Falls

Waterfalls and lakes may be common in Rocky Mountain National Park, but waterfall-lake combos like this one are surprisingly rare, so enjoy.

Start: Longs Peak Trailhead
Hiking time: 5 to 6 hours
Distance: 8 miles out-and-back
Difficulty: Easy to very strenuous
Other trail users: Human foot traffic only
Maps: Trails Illustrated #200: Rocky Mountain National Park; USGS Longs Peak
Highlights: Lake-waterfall combo, mountain views
Elevations trailhead to Peacock Pool and Columbine Falls: 9,400 feet to 11,570 feet (+2,170 feet)

Finding the trailhead: From the junction of US 36 and CO 7 in Estes Park, drive south on CO 7 for 9.2 miles and turn right on Longs Peak Road to parking and the trailhead (GPS: 40 16.2852, -105 33.3901).

The Hike

Peacock Pool, a smaller lake in the valley below Chasm Lake, is best viewed from the trail. The multihued pool is in a sensitive ecological area, so a trail doesn't descend to the lake, which is at 11,310 feet altitude, and visitation is discouraged to protect fragile alpine plants and avoid erosion. Admire it from a distance on your hike.

Starting at Longs Peak Trailhead, this hike follows the East Longs Peak Trail alongside sparkling Alpine Brook, passing twisted limber pines in Goblins Forest and Jims Grove to timberline and a major trail junction and toilet at 11,540 feet. Go left on Chasm Lake Trail for the hike's second leg. Contour west below the southeastern flank of Mount Lady Washington, edging above 100-foot-high Columbine Falls below the trail and giving views of Peacock Pool. If you have the energy, continue another 0.2 mile up to Chasm Lake and grand views of the Diamond on Longs Peak.

Miles and Directions

- **0.0** Start at the Longs Peak Trailhead at the south end of the parking lot and hike west on the East Longs Peak Trail.
- **0.5** Reach junction with Eugenia Mine Trail on the right. Keep left toward Chasm Lake and hike uphill to a bridge over Larkspur Creek. Continue to a bridge over Alpine Brook.
- **1.1** Junction with a spur trail to Goblins Forest Backcountry Campsite.
- **2.4** Junction with a spur trail to Battle Mountain Backcountry Campsite.
- **3.3** Arrive at a major junction with the Chasm Lake Trail and a toilet with a view at 11,540 feet. Go left on the signed Chasm Lake Trail and cross rocky slopes on the southeast flank of Mount Lady Washington.
- **4.0** Arrive at the overlook for Peacock Pool and Columbine Falls. (If you have the energy, continue to Chasm Lake.) Return the way you came.
- **8.0** Arrive back at the trailhead.

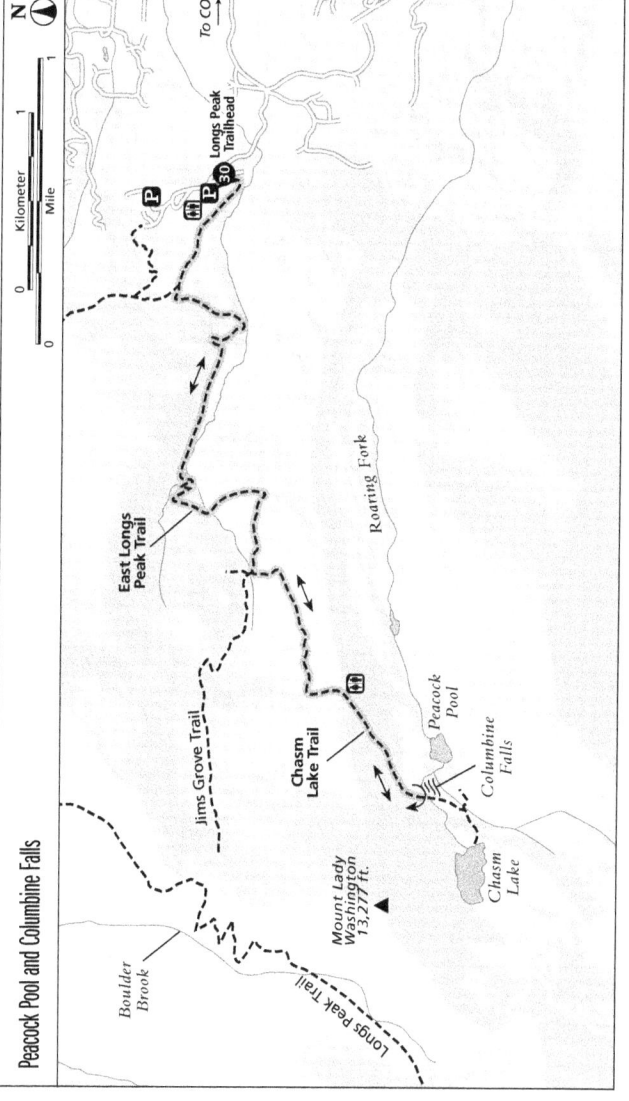

31 Cascade Falls and North Inlet Falls

North Inlet flows from Taylor Peak and Lake Nokoni, forming a series of waterfalls along the North Inlet Trail and providing a wonderous waterfall hike.

Start: North Inlet Trailhead
Hiking time: 10 to 12 hours
Distance: 15.4 miles out-and-back
Difficulty: Easy to very strenuous
Other trail users: Equestrians
Maps: Trails Illustrated Rocky Mountain National Park; USGS Grand Lake
Highlights: Waterfalls, North Inlet Creek
Elevations trailhead to North Inlet Falls: 8,510 feet to 9,490 feet (+980 feet)

Finding the trailhead: On US 34 approaching Grand Lake from the south, drive to a Y junction just south of the Grand Lake Visitor Center and bear right on West Portal Road / CO 278. Continue 0.3 mile and bear left to stay on West Portal Road. Drive 0.8 mile and turn left on CR 663. Continue 0.2 mile, past the Tonahutu Trailhead, then turn right and go 0.1 mile to parking and the trailhead (GPS: 40 15.412, -105 48.843).

The Hike

This waterfall-rich hike follows North Inlet Trail along a long, curving valley carved by ancient glaciers and North Inlet Creek in the southwest part of Rocky Mountain National Park. Hiking to all of these waterfalls is a major undertaking, and most hikers turn around at Cascade Falls, the first one, rather than continuing deep into the backcountry. If you plan on day hiking to see all six waterfalls, bring snacks, water, and rain gear, and start early. Parking at the

North Inlet Trailhead is limited, so if the lots are full, park at the bottom of the hill and hike to the trailhead.

Parts of North Inlet Trail were burned by the East Troublesome Fire in 2020. Check with the park before hiking for possible trail and area closures. The first waterwall is signed "Cascade Falls" and reached by a side trail on the right. Loop upstream to see the falls tumbling over dark boulders stacked in the creek bed. Past it is "Cascade Falls Point" on the left at 9,723 feet altitude and the upper rapids of the falls on the right. "Snake Dance Falls" gushes down a steep chute into a shallow plunge pool below. Farther up the trail is "Big Pool Falls," which drops into a large pool of frigid, shallow water. The waterfall's top is right of the trail. Note that the creek has carved scalloped edges into the bedrock below. Next is "Sun Dance Falls." Climb onto a broad rock above the waterfall for a closer look. After a footbridge, the trail reaches the long cascades of "Rain Dance Falls" and then an unnamed lake. War Dance Falls, which is not included in this hike's miles and directions, lies past North Inlet Group Campsite. The trail to it is faint and gains 340 feet of elevation—with no switchbacks. Best to skip War Dance and admire it from a distance. The hike's last waterfall, North Inlet Falls, is the best. The falls plunge in a gleaming, liquid curtain through a rocky gorge, with views on either side of the falls and from a bridge.

Take a good rest here before returning to the trailhead—you've earned it.

Miles and Directions

0.0 Begin at North Inlet Trailhead. Hike east down gravel road past private property and horse pastures.

3.5 Depart main trail and go right to Cascade Falls on short path. Return to main trail.

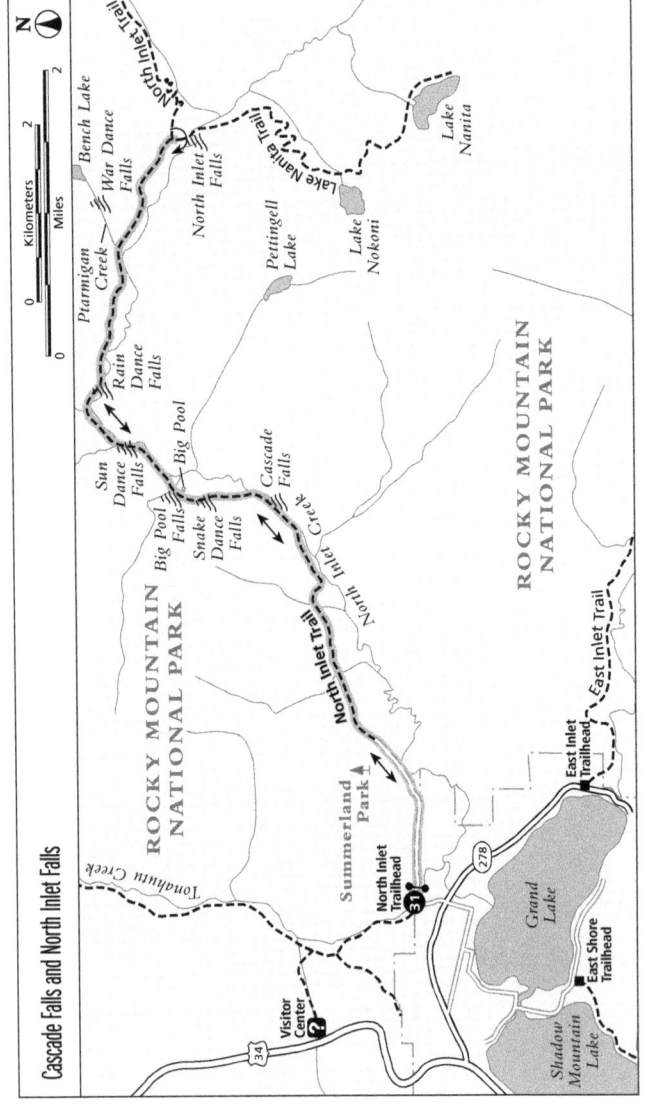

- **4.5** At a hard left switchback, step right off trail to see "Snake Dance Falls" dropping into a shallow plunge pool. Continue on main trail.
- **4.9** Arrive at "Big Pool Falls" to right of trail. Continue on main trail.
- **5.0** Pass Big Pool Campsite and reach "Sun Dance Falls" to right of trail. Continue on trail.
- **5.7** Cross a footbridge and arrive at "Rain Dance Falls" to right of trail. Continue on main trail.
- **6.7** Cross another footbridge and pass North Inlet Group Campsite to junction on left with rough trail that climbs to War Dance Falls (not part of this hike). Continue on main trail.
- **7.7** Reach trail junction. Left fork leads to Flattop Mountain and Bear Lake; keep right toward Lakes Nokoni and Nanita.
- **7.9** Arrive at North Inlet Falls (GPS: 40 16.734, -105 43.281). Return the way you came.
- **15.4** Arrive back at trailhead.

32 Adams Falls

A gentle trail leads to a misty falls within a spectacular defile.

Start: East Inlet Trailhead
Hiking time: 30 minutes to 1 hour
Distance: 1-mile lollipop loop
Difficulty: Very easy
Other trail users: Equestrians
Maps: Trails Illustrated #200: Rocky Mountain National Park; USGS Shadow Mountain
Highlights: Adams Falls
Elevations trailhead to Adams Falls: 8,400 feet to 8,450 feet (+50 feet)

Finding the trailhead: On US 34 approaching Grand Lake from the south, drive to a Y junction just south of the Grand Lake Visitor Center and bear right on West Portal Road / CO 278. Continue 0.3 mile and bear left to stay on West Portal Road. Drive 2 miles to parking and the trailhead, on left (GPS: 40 14.400, -105 48.018).

The Hike

The easy walk to Adams Falls rises gradually amid lodgepole pines and glacially deposited boulders. Adams Falls is within a gorge that evidently follows a geologic crack formed during the uplift of the Rockies and subsequently altered by glacial scouring and water erosion. Splashing through this defile, East Inlet Creek throws up much spray, which can form rainbows around the falls. To see a rainbow, you must have the sun behind you as you look at the water droplets in the air.

Rocks around Adams Falls are smooth, steep, and often wet, all of which contribute to treacherous footing. Parents should take care that their children do not slip into the stream and get washed over the brink.

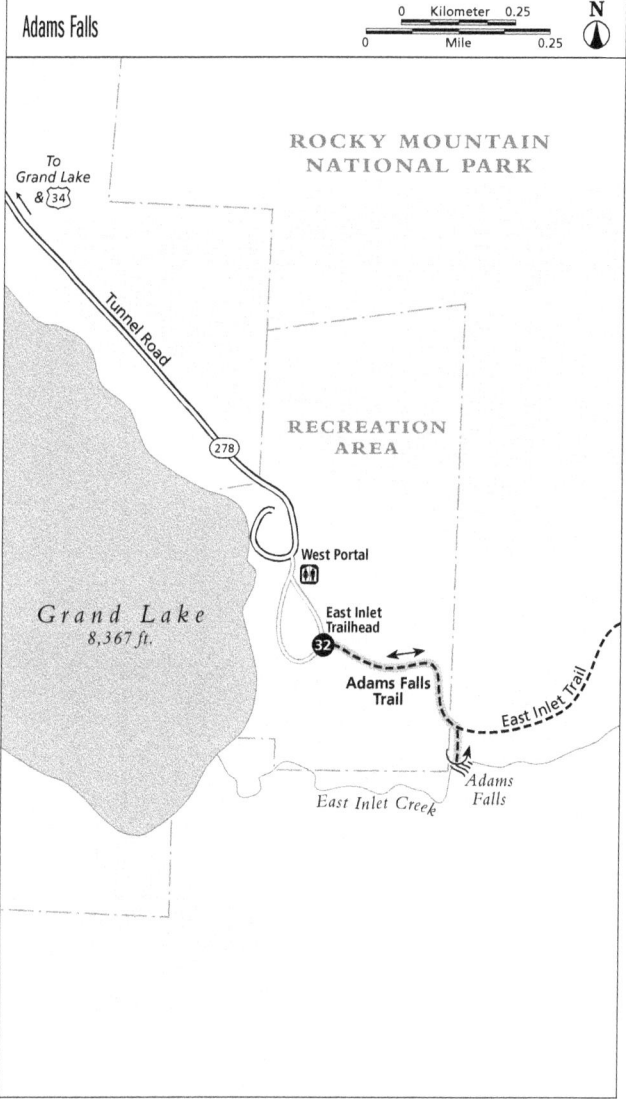

Miles and Directions

0.0 Begin at East Inlet Trailhead and hike southeast on trail.
0.3 Leave main trail at junction. Go right and descend stone steps on Adams Falls Trail, an 815-foot path, to reach viewing area for Adams Falls. Climb steps left of falls to return to East Inlet Trail.
0.5 Rejoin East Inlet Trail and turn left.
1.0 Arrive back at the trailhead.

33 Lone Pine Lake and Lake Verna

Two of Rocky Mountain National Park's most remote and lonesome lakes—Lone Pine Lake and Lake Verna—nestle in the narrow floor of a dramatic, glaciated valley on the rugged western slope of the Continental Divide.

Start: East Inlet Trailhead
Hiking time: 9 to 10 hours
Distance: 13.4 miles out-and-back
Difficulty: Easy to very strenuous
Other trail users: Equestrians
Maps: Trails Illustrated #200: Rocky Mountain National Park; USGS Shadow Mountain, Isolation Peak
Highlights: Lakes, mountain views
Elevations trailhead to Lake Verna: 8,400 feet to 10,180 feet (+1,780 feet)

Finding the trailhead: On US 34 traveling north toward Grand Lake, drive to a Y junction just south of the Grand Lake Visitor Center and bear right on West Portal Road / CO 278. Continue 0.3 mile and bear left to stay on West Portal Road. Drive 2 miles to parking and the trailhead, on left (GPS: 40 14.400, -105 48.018).

The Hike

A ladder of five lakes hides in a high, glacier-carved valley on the west side of Rocky Mountain National Park. The lowest lakes—Lone Pine Lake and Lake Verna—are reached by a long hike up the East Inlet Trail from Grand Lake. The higher lakes lie in the upper valley below the Continental Divide in one of the park's wildest and least visited places.

East Inlet, originating on the rugged north slope of Isolation Peak, dashes northwest down the deep valley, filling the lakes and splashing over waterfalls, before emptying into Grand Lake, Colorado's largest and deepest natural lake.

Visiting the two lower lakes is a major hike with plenty of miles and elevation gain. Plan on a long day, so bring food, water, a headlamp, extra clothes, and rain gear. Trekking poles and MICROspikes are essential if there is any chance that snow and ice cover the trail. Use caution on the narrow and exposed trail section above the rocky gorge and East Inlet Falls, especially in wet or snowy conditions.

A faint path continues past Lake Verna on this hike to Spirit Lake. To see the three highest lakes, book a wilderness campsite at Solitaire, Slickrock, Upper East Inlet, or Lake Verna to spend a starry night and explore them the next day.

Miles and Directions

- **0.0** Begin at the East Inlet Trailhead and hike southeast on the trail.
- **0.3** Reach a junction with a short trail that goes right down steps to a viewpoint of Adams Falls. Return to East Inlet Trail and go right, passing an alternative side trail that goes right to Adams Falls. Continue east, skirting along the northern edge of a wide meadow. Look for moose. Cross low hills and continue east, following the northern fringe of more meadows and wetlands along meandering East Inlet creek.
- **2.2** At the trail's second footbridge, step left to see Footbridge Falls, then continue east into wooded hills studded with cliffs.
- **3.0** The trail twists along a bench between cliffs before traversing an exposed, narrow section above a high cliff. Use extreme care and avoid loose, wet, or icy rock here. Exposure is extreme and a fall would be fatal. The creek dashes through a rock-walled gorge below the trail.
- **3.1** Reach a viewpoint of East Inlet Falls in the deep canyon below. Past here, make a switchback left and climb over a rounded granite dome, then head east on rocky benches and hills in a wide, glaciated valley.

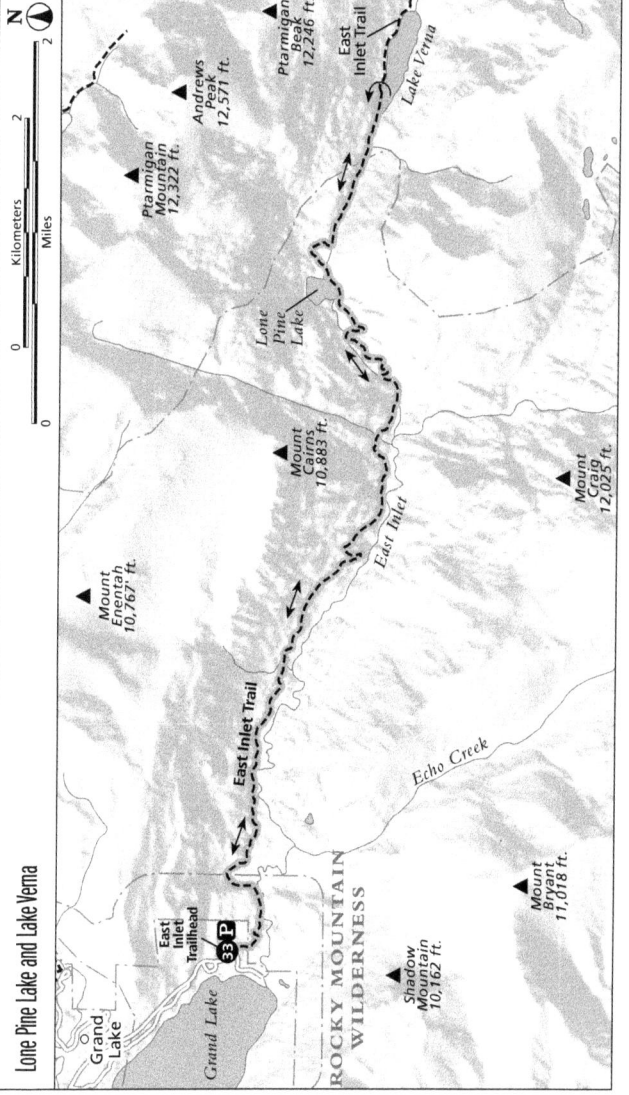

4.2 The trail crosses East Inlet and switchbacks northeast up a long rocky hill and then levels off, passing a small pond, and then climbing again.

5.3 Reach the southeast side of Lone Pine Lake below a high, slabby cliff covered with trees. After enjoying the pretty lake, head east of the lake through slickrock hills and then follow the creek's left side east up a narrow, rocky valley, passing the turn to East Inlet Backcountry Campsite just past a small lake formed by a landslide. Continue climbing to the narrow outlet bay of Lake Verna and hike along its north side.

6.7 Reach an open viewpoint on the north edge of Lake Verna. Look up the valley for dramatic views of the glaciated gorge to 13,114-foot Isolation Peak. More lakes hide in the upper valley—Spirit Lake, Fourth Lake, and Fifth Lake, tucked in the high cirque below Isolation Peak. After admiring the view, head back down the trail for the long hike out.

13.4 Arrive back at the trailhead.

About the Authors

Guidebooks by **Kent Dannen** are the standard reference for the trails of Rocky Mountain National Park. He hiked every trail in the park and those in this guide many times. Kent began his professional guiding activities as hike master and naturalist for the YMCA of the Rockies and led hundreds of hikes covering thousands of miles. He was a writer, photographer, and contributing editor of *Backpacker Magazine*, and he taught classes from coast to coast in nature photography, bird identification, and the history of wildlife in America for the National Wildlife Federation and Canadian Wildlife Federation. He also was a recipient of the US Department of Agriculture Certificate of Appreciation for his outstanding volunteer services in developing educational materials that help manage and protect the Indian Peaks Wilderness. His other guidebooks include *Short Hikes in Rocky Mountain National Park*, *Hiking Rocky Mountain National Park*, *Best Hikes Rocky Mountain National Park*, *Best Hikes Colorado's Indian Peaks Wilderness*, *Hiking Waterfalls Rocky Mountain National Park*, and *Rocky Mountain Wildflowers*. Kent died in 2025.

Susan Joy Paul has hiked, camped, and climbed all over Rocky Mountain National Park and throughout Colorado. An avid adventurer, she has summited more than 760 peaks including all of the Colorado 14ers. Susan was the first woman to summit every ranked peak in Colorado's El Paso County and Teller County and the thirty-sixth person to summit every Colorado county highpoint. Her memorable routes and peaks include the Keyhole Route on Longs Peak, the Knife Edge on Capitol Peak, the Maroon Bells Traverse, the Mountaineer's Route on Mount Whitney, the East Arête on Mount Russell, Otto's Route on Independence Monument, the Emmons Glacier on Mount Rainier, the Gooseneck Glacier on Gannett Peak, the Jamapa Glacier on Pico de Orizaba, the Ayoloco Glacier on Iztaccihuatl, and the Whymper Route on Chimborazo. Her books include *Touring Colorado Hot Springs* (2nd and 3rd editions); *Hiking Waterfalls Colorado* (1st and 2nd editions); *Climbing Colorado's Mountains*; *Best Lake Hikes Colorado*; *Woman in the Wild: The Everywoman's Guide to Hiking, Camping, and Backcountry Travel*; and *Trails to the Top: 50 Colorado Front Range Mountain Hikes*. Susan lives in Colorado Springs, Colorado.

FALCONGUIDES

MAKE ADVENTURE YOUR STORY™

Since 1979, FalconGuides has been a trailblazer in defining outdoor exploration. Elevate your journey with contributions by top outdoor experts and enthusiasts as you immerse yourself in a world where adventure knows no bounds.

Our expansive collection spans the world of outdoor pursuits, from hiking and foraging guides to books on environmental preservation and rockhounding. Unleash your potential as we outfit your mind with unparalleled insights on destinations, routes, and the wonders that await your arrival.

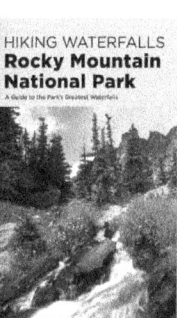

LET FALCON BE YOUR GUIDE

Available wherever books are sold.
Orders can also be placed at www.globepequot.com,
by phone at (800) 223-2336,
or by email at Purchaseorders@simonandschuster.com.

THE TEN ESSENTIALS OF HIKING

American Hiking Society

Whether you plan to be gone for a couple of hours or several months, make sure to pack these items. Become familiar with these items and know how to use them.

Find other helpful resources at AmericanHiking.org/hiking-resources

1. Appropriate Footwear

6. Safety Item (light, fire, and a whistle)

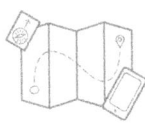
2. Navigation

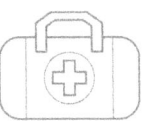
7. First Aid Kit

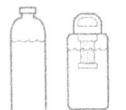
3. Water (and a way to purify it)

8. Knife or Multi-Tool

4. Food

9. Sun Protection

5. Rain Gear & Dry-Fast Layers

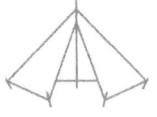
10. Shelter

PROTECT THE PLACES YOU LOVE TO HIKE

Become a member today and take $5 off an annual membership using the code **Falcon5**.

AmericanHiking.org/join

American Hiking Society is the only national nonprofit organization dedicated to empowering all to enjoy, share, and preserve the hiking experience.

www.ingramcontent.com/pod-product-compliance
Lightning Source LLC
LaVergne TN
LVHW051216070526
838200LV00063B/4930